Lovingly Abused

A true story of overcoming cults,
gaslighting, and legal educational neglect

Lovingly Abused

A true story of overcoming cults, gaslighting, and legal educational neglect

Heather Grace Heath

Charleston, SC
www.PalmettoPublishing.com

*Lovingly Abused: A true story of overcoming cults,
gaslighting, and legal educational neglect*

First Edition

Hardcover ISBN: 978-1-7378430-0-9
Paperback ISBN: 978-1-7378430-1-6
eBook ISBN: 978-1-7378430-2-3

To my sister,
who always asked me to make up just one more
"Penelope Story" before bed.

Contents

Author's Note

This is the true story of my own experience in an exclusive fundamentalist homeschool group. Those of us who have walked away, the backslidden or "Exers," as we call ourselves, each have our own unique version of this past life in a cult. I understand and acknowledge that although my story is traumatic, it comes from a place of privilege. My upbringing fueled the systemically oppressive behaviors for which I am guilty and will never be able to undo. My intention is never to invalidate the trauma of others nor direct attention away from those whose lives depend on our immediate action. In fact, stop reading and go do something that will make someone's life better and no one's life worse, then come back. I'll be here.

The abuse I experienced was mostly invisible to those right in front of me. It was invisible to my abusers. They thought they were doing what God wanted and, in doing so, became trapped themselves. My goal in writing this book is to open society's eyes to the hidden world of homeschoolers who are frequently dismissed as kind of weird but great at spelling bees. I'll show you how to recognize subtle warnings that a child needs a safe adult to intervene and how to help.

There are many points in this book readers may find triggering including, but not limited to:

Child abuse, sexual assault, pregnancy loss, suicide, divorce, racism, traumatic deaths, and I'm sure more that are so deeply ingrained into my thinking that I have yet to recognize them as triggers. Please always practice self-care and boundaries.

A percentage of the profits from this book are being donated to non-profits that advocate for the rights of children around the world who are denied access to education, through either financial, logistical, or religious oppression. Thank you for being part of the solution. You can find a list and more information in chapter 13 and at HeatherGraceHeath.com

Some of the names used in this book have been changed; most have taken on the form of pseudonyms to reflect the way they are seen in my mind.

Introduction

"Whosoever toucheth the dead body of any man that is dead, and puri-fieth not himself, defileth the tabernacle of the Lord; and that soul shall be cut off from Israel: because the water of separation was not sprinkled upon him, he shall be unclean; his uncleanness is yet upon him."

—Numbers 19:13

Have you ever been so haunted by childhood indoctrination that you pulled off a man's arm?

I have.

Well, not his entire arm, but pulling off more than none is too much.

It's moments like this—my heavy boots slowly attaching to the hallway carpet, soaked with the velcro-like fluid that finally alerted the neighbors to call 911—that make me feel like I'm existing in multiple timelines. My body stays in the present but the rest of me, I call her my Self, travels back and forth. It's as if my 33 years are on a Rolodex in my brain that's spun until my Self finds the moment most likely responsible for the origin of my thinking errors and fears that led me to this point. In an instant, I can feel the jolting crack of a Bible on a pulpit, flash-backs of sermons encompassing me, as I try to fight them out of my view so I can focus on what to do with the silhouette of a long, regal glove made from the skin I'm holding on the end of my EKG wire.

Figuring out how I got here is easy. Figuring out how to feel comfortable outside of a traumatic environment is the tricky part. Think about it: if you're brand new on the job and standing in a puddle of melting flesh as burly detectives yell at you for being in their way, your day probably isn't going to get worse. If there's anything that "Christians" love, it's having a terrible time—or, as they call it, "walking through trials" or "carrying a heavy burden" because it means that they are about to be blessed.

When everything seems to be perfect—like when I crawl into my daughter's bed to say goodnight but she wraps her snuggly-jams arms around my neck, getting her bracelets caught in my hair and, instead of wriggling free, I stay, terrified of this moment ever ending—that's when I'm most on guard. The Garden of Eden was perfect, Sodom and Gomorrah seemed to be a pretty fun place, and Job had the family and life of his dreams; they were all taken away in seconds because Satan had to go and fuck things up for the Believers. It didn't matter what words spewed from the preacher's mouth; all I heard was that if I was ever happy, it meant I should brace for a Spiritual Jumanji. I figured I could avoid Biblical levels of my faith being tested by not letting myself bask in the nanoseconds of perfection in life. I could keep myself safe if I managed to stay in crisis mode as much as possible.

I think that's why so many of us stayed silent about our abuse. Humans, raised in cults or not, are all driven by the reward center in our brain. We believed that the more we endured, the bigger the blessing, or reward, would be. If I've learned anything from 2020, it's that homeschooling on the other side now, as a working parent, is exhausting to endure. Accidental Homeschoolers of 2020, I applaud you. I was the heartbroken child kept from her friends and now I'm the parent who soothes her heartbroken children, who are now fluent in Zoom etiquette. I can finally, though reluctantly, acknowledge my parents' view that homeschooling was their Spiritual test. But there is a difference between avoiding a global pandemic and avoiding reality. That difference is where the abuse lies.

The most frightening thing about abuse in homeschooling households is that most of the parents have no idea what they are doing is abusive. A common thread I've found among the parents of us Exers is that they were trying so hard to protect us from the trauma of their childhood, they didn't see that they were robbing us of ours.

Every single time I encounter a child, my radar goes on full alert for warning signs that they are being lovingly abused by parents who are just as trapped. The signs are subtle, but it's my goal to use my story to teach you what to look for. I wish someone would have picked up on the signs when I was right in front of them, silently screaming for help between the sound of my poignantly scripted answers about how I was perfectly content with my baggy homemade dresses that fell to my ankles and blessed with parents who wanted to protect me by being my only friends. Most of my Self believed there was validity in the reasons my parents instructed me to give when grocery cashiers would ask me "What about socialization?"; I was a child, and children instinctively trust their parents. My kids believe that commercials are like Facebook for TV: "Yeah, the stuff exists, but it's not for you. Those people just want you to be happy for them." And if you're judging me for lying to my kids, let she who has never lied to a toddler cast the first stale car-floor chicken nugget.

But I don't think my parents knew they were lying. They truly believed they were raising me according to God's will, propagated by the community they believed to have rescued them.

Ironically, these families so against socialization were the very ones who created an international community so they wouldn't feel isolated by never leaving their homes.

My instinct to protect myself by remaining in crises combined with my insatiable need to break free from the fundamentalist patriarchy found a serendipitous career as a paramedic. Although I had physically disconnected by driving away and never looking back, the indoctrination deconstruction remains an ongoing battle. I was taught to believe that every single word of the King James Bible is true beyond a shadow of a doubt. I still have full chapters memorized. I fell asleep nightly to The Bible on cassette. When you leave a world that taught you everything you know, you're not starting with a blank foundation. You're starting with a skyscraper that needs to be replaced brick by brick, but you never know which brick will be pulled out next.

"You're responding for the welfare check/suspicious smell in the apartment," our dispatcher told us as we flipped on the sirens and headed to the call, annoyed that we'd have to wait to get our morning coffee. After the firefighter broke the door open, I saw him. He still resembled a person but every drop of life had drained out of his body and into the hallway. Although I'd been an EMT for six years and had been to morgues and funerals more times than I could count, this was different. This was the first time I encountered a dead body as a paramedic – the one responsible for announcing the time of declared death. I was shaking. Per my protocols, I could have presumed death with the obvious decomposition alone but I wanted to be thorough, in case my director wanted to see proof of death in my chart. I put the stickers that would snap to my EKG wires on his arms and legs, to show his absent heartbeat as a flat-line. I stood in the hallway, my partner off in the distance vomiting, as the pink-squared EKG paper printed out the lifeless tracing. Declared time of death: 6:03 am.

Fuck. Now what? I had to disconnect him from my monitor. Putting the stickers on him was okay in my mind because I hadn't yet declared him dead. But now he was officially dead. I felt as if I had sealed my own unclean fate; suddenly, the brick that forbade me from touching a dead body was yanked from my skyscraper.

As the blinding indoctrination swirled around me, I did the only thing I could think of. I stayed in the hall and pulled the wires off as hard as I could, hoping they would unsnap from the stickers as they had inconveniently done with dozens of other patients in the past. Three of the four unsnapped but one of the stickers caught his skin just right and, as I pulled, the skin from his arm and hand peeled off effortlessly, ending up inverted at the end of the wire nearest to my face. I'd have to touch the degloved skin to get it off my wire.

As we all began gagging, my mental Rolodex stopped on the fear of being marked unclean. At that moment, I knew this brick was only the beginning.

1

Learning the Language

There are going to be many points throughout this book when you may find you have no idea what I'm talking about and not know what a standard-to-me term means. That's a good thing.

Rather than include a glossary, I'm going to attempt to set you up for success by giving you a full rundown before you dive into my story. Honestly, this chapter is mostly for my husband and my therapists so I don't have to keep pausing to explain what I'm talking about. Some of the terms here didn't quite fit into the storyline but I feel are important to include so you can immerse yourself into the mindset without having to join a cult.

I'll advise there are some extremist labels for people and gender stereotypes used in my stories. I include these words not as my own, but to illustrate exactly how I was taught to see people and the hatred I had to overcome.

—**The Advanced Training Institute International**, aka **ATI**: What I'm referring to whenever I speak of "the cult." This is the private, fundamentalist homeschool organization in which I was raised. People often ask me what ATI is. The organization has physical locations for its headquarters and various "training centers," but ATI isn't a place; it's a program. This is how I was raised in Connecticut but am connected to the now famous quiverfull families you see on reality shows.

Originally ATIA, the second "A" (America) was changed to "I" in the early '90s when, according to the details I've been able to gather from friends who remember the switch, one of the girls Bill Gothard was grooming either lived in or moved to New Zealand, so the program became international, in order for Bill to keep her under his watch. My family didn't join until '97, when it was already ATII. Eventually, the only acceptable slang term we were allowed to use was "ATI" because everyone was too busy counting all of their children to say a second "I."

ATI is now unfortunately used in over a dozen countries. This is the organization responsible for our entire curriculum, training conferences, newsletters, mission trips, spiritual guidance, and the strict behavioral standards set for members.

—**ALERT**, the "Air Land Emergency Resource Team": Basically, this team got to do all the exciting stuff. If there was ever a part of ATI I'm bummed I missed, it's this. I'd never encourage anyone to embrace ALERT now but, if I had to be raised in a cult, I'd rather have been a part of the program that actually did something productive. Every year, our giant conference would start with ALERT guys rappelling down in front of the American flag. I put "rappelling" on my to-learn list, but had one of my first deaths-of-a-vision (you'll get to that in the Ds) when they said I couldn't rappel in a skirt. Yeah, obviously, so I'll grab some pants. Well, that was when I discovered that changing my clothes wasn't an option on their radar and that "skirt" was a stop point for them. ALERT is enough of an established response team that they have their own ambulance. Of the dozens of oppressive ATI programs, this is the most justifiable to society.

—**Altar-filling**: A sermon so Spiritually convicting the altar (usually the front of a stage or platform) is filled with rows of tearful sinners. I was unaware until final edits that The World thinks altar-filling means booking a speaker. Silly World, that's pulpit-filling.

—**Appearance of Evil**: 1 Thessalonians 5:22 states "Abstain from all appearance of evil." ATI loves this verse because it doesn't take much effort at all to make it mean whatever they'd like. Basically, it's anything that could cause a rumor to start or a person to think you find something permissible when, in fact, you do not.

This is why men and women are never to be alone together and why, if a woman needs to contact a married man, his wife must always be part of the conversation. If a man needs to contact a woman, her father, brother, or husband must be a part of the conversation.

ATI families may not attend movies in a theatre, even if it is a G-rated kids' film. The reasoning is that someone may see the family at the theatre and assume they are going to a sinful film, causing that person to decide to fall into sin, as well. Unmarried men and women may never ride alone in a car together, nor sit next to each other in a church service without leaving ample room for Jesus between their hips.

When I was 7, I had a massive crush on a boy at church. We used to share a hymnal until we were made to stop because that was hardcore flirting (which we knew and was why we were sharing). If only they had stopped us sooner, he probably wouldn't have taught me how to milk his goat later that year (not a euphemism). I apologize to any other students in our Sunday School class who we may have led astray with our provocative goat-milking, hymnal-sharing behavior.

—**Basic Seminar/"The Basic"**: Where it all began, in 1964, with the peak being in the '80s. The Basic was Bill Gothard's first seminar, offering victory over "youth conflicts," such as immorality, rock music, bitterness, and rebellion. The Basic is the foundation of all the cult's teachings and everyone over age 12 is required to attend at least once in order to enroll in ATI. Many families attend or host a Basic at least yearly, if not more frequently.

My parents can quote the Basic the way many of my friends can quote The Office. Once you've attended a Basic, you are eligible to attend The Advanced Seminar. Both parents enrolling in ATI must attend an Advanced in order to be accepted. It is up to the parents to determine when each of their children (over 12) is ready to attend an Advanced.

—**Birth of a Vision**: An Idea. Honestly. The only difference between a vision and an idea is that ideas come from the human mind, and visions come from God. A vision is a little more intense than a rhema, but not as much of a life-long commitment as a calling. Birth of a Vision is the point when the idea begins to form. Rarely does the vision come to fruition without several obstacles thrown at you from the Devil. There are levels to this which I'll explain once you get to death of a vision.

—**Blanket Training**: I didn't fully remember the details, so my mother helped fill in some of the blanks on this one. Blanket training was done by thousands of ATI families but no one ever talked about it outside of our private conferences. One of the mothers who sat on the "Mother's Panel" beside the wretch who trained all the other mothers in how it's done even managed to be the star of a popular reality show, complete with scandals and abuse accusations, but never openly revealed the practice of Blanket Training. Keeping it covered up was no accident (although that pun was). Everyone knew that "the world" would see such parenting behavior as "extreme" and would likely provoke government suspicion. I'm glad that, finally, there are articles exposing such abuse, which you can find with a quick internet search.

Blanket training is the practice of training a child, preferably a small baby, to remain on a single blanket and entertain themselves with a few toys. The blanket is meant to replace a playpen for convenience and establish outright obedience from day one. To begin blanket training, you would place your baby on the blanket, near the edge, and wait for them to move a limb past the edge of the blanket. Many parents start this training before their baby is even able to crawl and, in those cases, the parent is instructed to move the limb of the baby off the blanket for them, in order to establish the rules. Once the baby's limb crosses the edge, the parent is to slap the offending limb and move it back to the blanket. This type of lab rat conditioning continues until the baby learns that straying from the blanket equals pain, willingly inflicted by their only source of care.

I'm very grateful my mother did not fall prey to the teachings of blanket training. Because she refused to force an immobile baby to move their body just so she could slap them, she was seen as a hypocrite who did not take training the future generation seriously. I assume this is why I turned out to be the rebellious, equality-loving, authority-questioning, backslidden harlot I am today. One year at our conference, my mother was working the family viewing registration table and had my sister next to her on a blanket that looked like a dollhouse. The father from the popular reality show, who was at the time only "famous" for being an Arkansas State Representative, noted how well my sister played on the blanket and praised my mother for such a devoted blanket training example. The truth was my sister didn't like sharing her toys and really liked being close to our mom, which happened to be everything she needed from that blanket. In case you missed it, I'll tell that anecdote another way: a sitting elected official openly praised my mother because he thought she was practicing child abuse. Research who gets your vote!

—**Calling**: Your career, whether it's what you are passionate about doing OR the last thing on Earth you would want to do, yet signs from God keep coming to you, calling to a line of service. Men are called to be pastors or missionaries and, if they go into these careers without being called of God, they might as well not even get out of bed. We are taught in our Wisdom

Booklets that even if you are doing a good thing, if you aren't doing it because God wants you there, it's flatout sinful. Women are called to be wives, but sometimes specifically to be the wives of pastors or missionaries. That means if a woman falls in love with an astronaut, it's not God's will for them to be married, unless she had been called to marry a man with that career. Just kidding. Women aren't called to marry astronauts; astronauts believe in too much science. If a woman is called to pastor a church, it's easy to tell right from the start that this "calling" is false and straight out of the pit of Hell.

—**Chalk Talk**: A sermon given whilst drawing with chalk. Think "Mary Poppins Chimney Sweep" but with zero dancing and far less fun. Seeing a chalk talk live was like scoring tickets with an original Broadway cast. Most chalk talks were given by Bill but, as time went on, he started training the students in this art. There were specific pairings of sermons and drawings, and we had a print of "Psalm 1" which we intentionally displayed in the background of my ATI student photo. When your oppressor demands humility you find creative ways to humble brag. Only the most conviction-producing sermons were promoted to chalk talks.

—**Children's Institute**: The kids' version of The Basic. There is never a CI without a Basic and/or an Advanced, and children are only able to attend if their parent is also attending one of the seminars. Since all CIs are live (unlike the adult seminars, which are often recorded), ATI has a traveling team of Song Leader (always a female), Story Teller (always a male), and Piano Player (either cisgender). From about age 7 to 18, my life centered around CIs, thanks to my parents' unwaivering sacrifices to fuel that passion.

—**Church**: This is where I will debunk the claim that ATI is a church. Very often, an outsider will confuse the two, but they are more like a Venn diagram of organizations. The main difference is a church has one set of beliefs and is responsible for a person's spiritual wellbeing. ATI is "responsible" for education and has members of several religious denominations, such as: Amish, Baptist, Calvinist, Christian-Jews, Evangelical, Mennonite, Protestant, River Brethren, and non-denominational Christian. I have never heard of Catholics being involved in ATI. ATI does not hold worship services, but does center their teachings around the Bible and incorporates prayer into every message. In my experience ATI best aligns with the beliefs of Independent Fundamental Baptists (IFBs). All ATI families are required to be faithful church attendees, but ATI understands that many of their families are spiritually superior to the average church member, so many ATI families not only homeschool, but home church, as well.

—**Countenance Enhancing**: Women held full responsibility for whether or not their bodies caused a man to sin, including provoking impure thoughts. Frumpy clothes were not enough, so we were required to do at least three things to bring attention to our countenance, meaning our faces. Makeup was allowed as long as it enhanced the non-sinful features, such as cheeks, and did not cross over into temptress with smokey eyes and sultry lips. One set of earrings (the only piercings allowed) shorter than one inch long or half-inch hoops, glasses, necklaces that fell above your cleavage, and a constant smile also made the list. Oh, and neck-bows. I can enhance the shit out of a neck-bow. ATI never praises beauty but you could veil your compliment by stating how the joy of The Lord shone through her successful attempts of drawing attention to her face. Big hair and artistic french braids were all the rage.

I will say, many of the young women on ATI's staff were objectively gorgeous, which was partially attributed to these rules, but I later learned it was mostly because Bill handpicked his favorites as staff members. He favored blonde, bouncy curls, and thankfully I had not yet discovered how to scrunch out my crunch.

—**Courtship**: A couple enters into a courtship once their fathers determine the two are spiritually compatible, and the couple agrees the only thing that will end their courtship is their marriage. Dating is strictly forbidden in ATI. We're told courtship is for covenants, and dating is for divorce. They use the word "covenant" and not "commitment" because a covenant mirrors God's binding promises that cannot be broken. Since breaking up is a normal part of dating, we're taught this puts us in the mindset that if we aren't happy, we can leave. Dating is the choice of the individuals, while courtship involves active participation of paternal authority. Courtship is only for heterosexuals, and anyone in the LGBTQ+ community is sent to conversion camp (not hyperbole). A couple is always chaperoned to assure there is no physical contact, although some of the more liberal families allow side-hugs and hand hold-ing, as long as your fingers stay together. Interlaced fingers would be too slippery a slope into temptation.

I asked people what part of ATI makes them the most curious, and "dating"/"finding a spouse" was the most popular answer. I couldn't fit everything into this definition, so courtship ended up with its own chapter, "Satan's Doorbell."

—**Cult**: I am often asked why I say I was raised in a cult. The easy answer is that I was. A cult is often a religion, but doesn't need to be. Merriam-Webster defines a cult as, "[A] religion regarded as unorthodox or spurious," (spurious is my all-time favorite word for describing exactly what ATI is: "outwardly similar or corre-sponding to something without having its genuine qualities") and Dictionary.com defines cult as, "[A] relatively small group of people having religious beliefs or practices regarded by others as strange or sinister." When I refer to "The Cult," I am referring to ATI. Some people assume I mean the church my father still attends, yet I left after an extremely horrific cover-up of pedo-philia. I am incredibly intentional with my words and, although I did experience damaging practices and teachings in that church, including when a woman tried to exorcise my demons after I had a seizure, I personally do not consider it to be a cult in and of itself.

—**Death of a Vision**: This is an expected disappointment that soon follows a birth of a vision and is a solid confirmation that your vision is part of God's Will. A death of a vision does not take place when the visionary changes their mind, but rather when an outside force appears to be making the vision impossible.

Not to worry, though. Soon to follow are: rebirth of a vision, double death of a vision, double rebirth of a vision, and so forth, until all trials are overcome and the vision is complete. Skipping from birth of a vision right to completion is much like Schwartz jumping right to the triple dog dare when he wanted to see if Flick's tongue would stick to the pole; you can do it, but it's highly frowned upon by all of your cohorts.

—**Energy Giver/Taker**: You've probably experienced this one. An energy giver is someone who is enthusiastic, motivating, and gets you in a better mood with just their presence. An energy taker is someone who drains every ounce of motivation you once had, such as the coworker who won't do anything unless it absolutely needs doing or the person who always accepts help but never gives it.

—**Excel**: The opposite of ALERT. According to their website, the world puts ungodly pressure on women to be independent when, in reality, they should be learning how to prepare for their role as a wife and mother. Young ladies aged 16 and older are encouraged to spend three thousand dollars to attend a five-week program on designing a home, housekeeping, hygiene, diet, journaling, calligraphy, basic first aid, and vehicle care (read: how to pump gas and check the oil). I think that now they are allowed to learn to change a tire. I can only imagine the hours of prayerful consideration it took to add such a masculine task to the syllabus.

—**Exers**: The way former ATI students refer to themselves and each other. An Exer differs from an alumni, in that an alumni may still agree with the teachings of ATI, while an Exer, like myself, spends a great deal of time constantly relearning how to view the world around them. All Exers are alumni, not all alumni are Exers.

—**Family Viewing**: This was the area at conferences where parents and siblings could sit to watch the session on a monitor while their infants and toddlers played quietly on their blankets. Breastfeeding was not allowed in family viewing or anywhere outside of the nursing mother's room. Even in the nursing mother's room, you were required to be fully covered. Ditching covers would bring the room a little too close to lesbianism, and we wouldn't want women getting the idea that it's acceptable not to answer to a man. Clearly, anyone who has ever breastfed knows that all you can think about while feeding your kid is how tempted you are to sin via the nourishing breasts surrounding you. My sister was most likely the oldest kid in the nursing mother's room, not because ATI is in favor of early weaning, but because most of the kids had to get bumped off so the next one could eat.

—**Head Covering**: It's always so funny to me when people mistake Mennonite for Amish. I was often mistaken for both, which was hilarious to me since I never wore a head covering. It's incredibly easy to tell different groups apart by their head coverings. Each sect has specific coverings, sometimes with different meanings within the sect. River Brethren's coverings look nothing like Amish or Mennonite coverings to us. Many women wore a small circle of cloth pinned to their head in obedience to their husband or father, but not tied to a conviction from their sect's beliefs.

—**Hedge Of Protection**: Kind of like sage smudging, but with a Bible. Any time someone is about to embark on a journey or challenge, their authority would pray a hedge of protection around them. When I arrive on scene of a crash, I ask "Were you wearing your seatbelt properly?", if something went wrong in ATI, the first question was whether or not a hedge had been prayed around you or not.

—**Home Church**: This is exactly what it sounds like: ATI families often found themselves too Spiritual for local churches and would create their own. Sometimes, home churches are shared by a few families, but ours consisted of just us getting up early on Sundays to listen to my father read from "Spurgeon's Sermons" while I counted the chevron lines on our orange and brown throw pillows.

—**Home Industry**: ATI forbids wives from working outside the home, with few exceptions. However, they do encourage women to create a home industry, which can be an MLM (Usborne is popular because they aren't focused on appearance) or a useful craft—think Etsy without the internet. Even years after leaving the cult I found myself drawn to MLMs. It's not a coincidence that many MLMs are based on religious foundations. I was drawn to Thirty-One because their business model is the Virtuous Woman, and I didn't join LuLaRoe because I knew it was a Mormon company and I couldn't figure out why everyone was cool with dressing modestly all of a sudden. It was highly triggering. I was good at them, and it felt natural until I discovered MLMs were my nicotine patches for cults; only I'd replaced soul-winning with sales, and an umbrella for an up-line.

—**IBLP**: The "**Institute in Basic Life Principles,**" created by Bill Gothard in 1964, the tree from which all his programs branch. ATI is one of the branches, and many programs like Character First!, ALERT, and Excel require ATI membership. The Basic and Advanced seminars (and Children's Institute) are some of the branches that don't require membership. This is how you will find many IBLP adjacent deconstructionists who were not in ATI.

—**Knoxville**: To most people, it's just a city. To ATI families, it's where all the magic happens. Every June, ATI would rent UT's entire campus and we would just take over. It was the only time in most of our lives that we would ever experience living in a dorm. After a year or so, we became pros on how to make the most of campus life. ATI headquarters would assign families to dorms, but my mother would always end up calling and getting us into Clement Hall, the one closest to the dining hall and shuttle bus stop. Once we parked our minivan, it stayed there for the duration of our adventure, although we often couldn't find it in the sea of 15-passenger vans required by most families. You know that Birth of a Vision you get when you find the last open spot in a lot, only to experience an instant Death of a Vision when you discover a motorcycle is there? That's what our minivan did to a bunch of fellow ATIers.

ATI held annual training conferences in San Jose and Knoxville, but Knoxville was Jacob and San Jose was Esau. Or, I should say, everyone liked Knoxville better and we didn't hide our favor. Knoxville meant conferences and classes from dawn to late night. The sleep deprivation was no accident. There were huge evening sessions and days were filled with programs for each member of the family. The male children (ages 6 to 17) went to ALERT, which was the coolest thing that existed in my Knoxville world. The ALERT guys got to rock climb and rappel, and practice search and rescue. I knew I would be fantastic at all of that, but girls weren't allowed.

I went with the female children (ages 6 to 11) to Pre-EXCEL, where we did crafts and sang at nursing homes. Sometimes, we would have lunch in the field next to where ALERT was running their drills. I created a small mutiny in my group, insisting that the boys got to do cooler things. My team leader ended up making a marching rhyme for us, like the boys were using: "I don't know what you've been told, but our girls can be very bold. Hiking up our skirts to run, we are having all the fun." It was zero fun having to be extremely conscious to hike up our skirts only high enough to avoid tripping, without showing more than the tops of our ankles. When I was older, I graduated to COMMIT (for female children, ages 12 to 17). It was here where I learned how to "date" Jesus. We learned how to enhance our countenance and care for our younger siblings as if they were our children, because God gave them to us so we could practice being wives.

—**Leader in Training**, or **LIT**: This is what ATI labeled the "ne'er-do-wells," as Bill referred to them. ATI never labeled anything with negative words, but if anything was followed by "in training," there was a pretty good chance it meant "not currently compliant." LITs were the teenagers who refused to adhere to ATI's standards and were "out from under the umbrella of authority." The worst of the LITs are sent to a training center in Indiana. From what I've heard, it's juvie for homeschoolers, but includes sentences for offenses such as drinking, addiction to rock music, tattoos, and homosexuality. It amazes me how many people don't know that conversion camps for minors exist.

You could also be sent to The LIT Center if you had committed an actual crime that had not been reported to the police because your parents/church leaders/ATI staff felt the "world" has too strict a punishment for pedophiles/molesters/incestual rapists, since the "world" never placed blame on the scantily-clad victim. If ATI becomes aware of such an incident, the victim is instructed to work through a series of studies, in order to determine the role they played, ask forgiveness for defrauding an otherwise Godly man, causing him to backslide, and later learn to see how many blessings she would have missed had she not been raped. I have a brochure about it.

—**Neck Bow**: The all-time favorite accessory of ATI teens, essential for letting a bit of their personality show amidst oceans of navy and white. A neck bow is sort of like a bow tie for women. However, women could not wear bow ties, as that was something that "pertaineth to a man." I was partial to the 1950s style of a short silk scarf tied in a knot off to one side. Every time I would make a skirt, I bought a little extra fabric, so I could make a matching neck bow. Since the World has ignored the Godly accessory of neck bows, if you wanted to find one in a store, it was best to look for the biggest, fluffiest barrette they had, replace the clip with a pin and wear it in your collar gap over your fastened top button. A few times, I went a little too big for ATI's standards and was admonished for my prideful neck bows. I have no neck bow regrets.

—**Parent Guide Planner**: These came with every Wisdom Booklet, in order to direct the mothers how to teach the lessons that month. My mother assumed teacher training would take place in Knoxville, but soon learned it was all preaching, no teaching.

—**Preacher Boy**: These are teen/college-aged boys who have been "called to preach." These boys tend to be the storytellers of a group and the ones who grow up to be the storyteller on the CI traveling team. I would have been in this category, if not for my prohibitive vagina. Preacher boys are the Danny Zukos of cults; hence, I found myself unmistakably called to be a preacher's wife.

—**Rhema**: A portion of Scripture brought to your attention by The Holy Ghost, or a vision (thought with a goal, not a hallucination) God has placed on your heart and then confirmed via signs or further Scriptures. ATI uses the examples of Mary learning she would give birth to Jesus and Peter learning he would deny Jesus thrice before dawn. More common forms of rhemas came in the form of "being led" to homeschool or deciding whether to leave/join a church or start your own (if you were a man). Note: We were taught that a woman would not receive a rhema requiring a life-changing event for a man. However, a man's rhema could determine the path of a woman's life, provided he is her "authority." I used to read my Bible over and over just hoping to get a rhema. As my favorite therapist put it: "I feel like you just described a spiritual orgasm."

—**Spiritual Cleanse**: If anyone experienced turmoil in their lives and couldn't figure out why, ATI would suggest going through a spiritual cleanse. These cleanses tend to go in waves, with the strongest being during or right after a conference. So many ATI families have terrible credit scores because they keep cutting up their cards and then later having to reapply for new ones.

Cleanses can range in intensity, and can be a family or individual activity. Sometimes, there is fasting. To begin, the father (obvi) leads the family through the house in search of anything that might cause one of the family members to sin. A lot of Disney movies would get tossed during these cleanses; while some children might have a take-away message from Winnie the Pooh to be kind to others, another child might embrace Eeyore's example and believe that depression is a chemical imbalance and not a conscious choice to reject joy. A spiritual cleanse is all or nothing. If an item causes one family member to sin, no one can have it. "Sheffey," the story of "A circuit-riding preacher named Robert Sheffey ministers to Appalachian mountain folk," was a popular movie in our circles, until a Family Coordinator dropped in on friends of ours and one of the kids quoted the line, "Fetch me my liquor, woman, before I beat ya senseless!" Sheffey was removed from the underground approved list, but that line became the inside joke when a woman wasn't being as submissive a wife as she should be. (It was "funny" because no one was allowed to have alcohol, ever, but we ended up using it as a metaphor for every situation of delayed spousal disobedience.)

—**Spiritual Gift**: Much like an Enneagram number or Myers-Briggs-type personality category, ATI highlights seven Spiritual gifts: Prophet, Server, Mercy, Exhorter, Teacher, Giver, and Organizer. Everyone took the SG test. I remember my parents breaking out the Basic seminar textbooks every time we had company, so they too could know which they were. My parents would make a party game of it, mixing up the questions so our guests wouldn't try to skew the results. My aunt once determined the Spiritual gifts of each Winnie the Pooh character, which technically wasn't allowed because no one was supposed to assume the Spiritual gift of another, but we decided it was ok because they were cartoons. Moderately tempered people tended to be teachers, exhorters, or givers. Organizers and servers leaned more towards hyperactive tendencies, controlling the only things in their lives they could control. Mercies were mostly the submissive mothers who had given up all will to fight, and prophets gave zero fucks. I always tested neck-in-neck with server/prophet but was labeled as "Server," because I'm a girl and they didn't need me fueling my unstoppable fire any further.

There's a rule in ATI that you always praise someone rather than insult them. For example, if someone was a complete asshole to you at a seminar, you could say, "Wow, you are really expressing your God-given prophetic reasoning tonight, huh?" Or if someone is constantly mansplaining things to you, you would let them know you'll remember to thank God later for sending such an exhorter into your life.

—**Spiritual Leader**: You'd think this would be summed up with "Pastor," but it's not. Men are the Spiritual leaders for their wives and children. If the family was attending a church, the Pastor was the Spiritual leader for the father. If the wife wanted to seek advice from the Pastor, she first had to talk to her husband. If guidance was still needed on the issue, he could go to the Pastor with his wife's message. Women could be the Spiritual leaders for other women and children, but never for a grown man, even her son.

—**Stronghold**: An area of your heart you have given over to Satan. The visual aide they always used was a grid that should have been controlled by God. Once a person becomes angry or bitter without asking God to quell these feelings, ground is given over to Satan and there is great Spiritual warfare in reclaiming the ground. Think castling but with demons instead of a rook.

—**Training Center**: ATI has several physical locations scattered throughout the U.S., Australia, New Zealand, and Romania, each with a different purpose or "a testimony of God's provision and direction," according to ATI's catalog. Training centers focus mostly on students ages 14 to 21, since that's the window most likely for rebellion. While most of ATI's teachings are done at home, the training centers are where kids are sent for a little more conditioning than their parents or church can give.

There are training centers for: ALERT; Excel; COMMIT; Sound Foundations—band camp; Journey to the Heart—nine days of prayer and meditation; Rise Up (not inspired by Hamilton)— where you "tackle the real-life relationship questions we all face, and gain a vision for how to live with a Kingdom mindset and an eternal perspective"; Quest—where boys learn to "put away childish things and choose Christlike manhood"; Character First!— where I went to be discovered for the Children's Institute traveling team; Telos—where students earned credits towards a degree (no longer active); Verity college—for students who insisted on having a paper that proved they were capable, rather than relying on God to impart this knowledge to future employers; Headquarters— staffed by ATI families and students. I was told you could not apply to live/work at headquarters; Bill Gothard had to inform you that God was leading you to serve with him. It's no coincidence that HQ was mostly staffed by single women who nailed the countenance-enhancing concept.

—**Umbrella of Authority**: The most oppressive symbol ATI created and the story behind my cover photo. In the "famous" diagram, we are shown that our authorities hold an umbrella of authority. (This was later changed to an umbrella of protection to make it under some abuse radars.) Mothers hold an umbrella over the children, fathers have one over the mothers, and God has the top umbrella. If you stray from under the umbrella, you are no longer able to benefit from the protection of your authority and disaster can strike. I have no idea why there needs to be three umbrellas stacked up when everyone could be just as dry under God's giant umbrella.

—**Wisdom Booklet**: This is the actual ATI curriculum. We never had grades in school. If someone asked what grade I was in, I always had to ask my mom what the answer should be. ATI kids went by which WB they were on. Every family starts at the first booklet, no matter the ages or time of joining. The idea is to study one WB a month, but there were some energy takers out there who took three months to get through one. Each WB was a continuation of the one previous, so the page numbers went from 1 to 3,000. By asking what WB someone was on (assuming they stayed on schedule), you could figure out how long they had been in ATI. The entire family studied the same WB, so some kids didn't start with the first if they were born into a family already working through them. Once you had finished all 54, you were to start back from one again until "graduation," whether you were around for the first time through or not.

—**Wisdom Search**: Daily devotions, ideally to be done as a family at dawn, led by the father. If a woman had a newborn, she was generally allowed to skip Wisdom Searches for about a month, which I assume was ATI's version of maternity leave. Part of the reason I wanted to have a ton of kids was the blissful idea of sleeping through a Wisdom Search. We also had personal WS and, at the training centers, we had groups and took turns leading. After my turns to lead, I usually ended up with a heart check because my rhemas were a bit too forward-thinking to have truly come from a place of Godly insight.

—**Wisdom Walk**: Essentially a "time-out" for kids with behavioral issues to be disciplined in the absence of the parent/authority. ATI forbade hitting/slapping/spanking by anyone other than the child's parent, so Wisdom Walks were the punishment used at children's seminars. One male would be assigned to WW, rather than a teaching team. He would walk around the seminar to see if there was a disruptive child or if a teacher had stuck "the hand sign" to the board, which meant a child on that team needed a Wisdom Walk. The Wisdom Walker would then bring that child to a quiet area to talk and pray about their behavior. Even though the Walker couldn't hit us, we knew we'd be hit at home once our umbrella holder found out.

I held a perfect track record for never getting one until WWs allegedly changed from being a punishment to just individual attention and they tried to get me to go. I wasn't falling for it, especially since I knew the teacher wasn't happy with my version of what counts as a stronghold. I knew they veiled negativity by twisting language and I wasn't about to get hit at home for nothing.

—**The World**: Anyone who thought differently from those leading ATI—even most churches—were referred to as "The World"-Defined by ATI as a noun: "The World would have us believe that women are equal to men. The World wants us to accept sodomy as a way of life. The World is convinced that education is the most important thing you can do for a child's future." I don't believe The World is inherently bad. Yes, everyone sins. The World does do terrible things. But The World pulled me out of misogynistic, manipulative, hateful captivity and taught me how to love with an open mind, finally separating faith from fascism.

—**Vain Repetitions**: A non-inspired prayer. Prayer was supposed to be 100% improv, and anything recited was an insult to

God. We knew The Lord's Prayer, but it was either recited as Scripture meditation or used as a guide to our own improv rather than a prayer we were to recite. We spent a lot of time throwing shade at Catholics for their vain repetitions.

2

Were Your Parents Always in a Cult?

"A father must be a rebuilder, no matter what his past failures may have been... When sons and daughters react to their father, they become just like him either in actions, or attitudes, or both. What fathers allow in moderation, their sons and daughters tend to excuse in excess."

—Men's Manual vol. 1

The roadmap leading to the cult is a bit blurred, since all I have to go on is what I've been able to piece together over the years. I've come to understand that the short answer is: "God led our family here." However, even extremists know that God doesn't act as our puppetmaster. There are always choices set before you and it is up to you how to act on them.

Most people I encounter think I was homeschooled due to religious standards; that's what we used as our reason. Some might say it was due to the fear of dangers that tragically threaten all grades, although violence was much less of an issue in the early 90s. Others may guess that my parents wanted to prepare me for advanced education, pressuring me to attend college early and build a successful career at a young age. That would make the most sense when joining a homeschooling cult, no?

But the truth is that after a ton of therapy - and finding out more and more about my mother's past - I realized that the reason for my sheltered life was none other than separation anxiety and cycles of Stockholm-ish self-sabotage.

My parents didn't always plan on homeschooling me. I have a video of my third birthday party where my mom was talking to cousins about becoming the bus driver or cafeteria worker, so she wouldn't have to be without me when I was at school. That wasn't about me. My kids are 5 and I'm already torn between counting down to the first day and sobbing over how much I'll miss them when kindergarten finally starts. They would have gone to pre-school, but the pandemic changed that. I'm not worried that they won't be ready and neither was my mom. I once went to a Breakfast with Santa at my grandfather's club and Santa was late. At 3 years old, I got up on stage and sang to the audience until Santa arrived. There was no fear that I couldn't make it on my own. The fear was that my mother would lose her purpose in life if I were gone.

It comes as a shock to most people that both of my parents attended public schools and had a (mostly) positive experience doing so. They attended the same high school, where my mother was a freshman when my father was a senior. My father went on to the Connecticut School of Broadcasting and eventually became a radio DJ. My mother earned a Bachelors of Fine Arts from UCONN, where she became heavily invested in the religious clubs. .

But that's the thing. No matter the lack of education or high level of degree, everyone has an innate longing to be accepted, and if we are promised happily ever after our judgement becomes blurred, leading us to sell our voice to a sea witch or our autonomy to a cult leader. The more trauma and suffering a person has experienced, the greater the desire for comfort and protection, with little thought to how much of oneself must be sacrificed.

As far as I know, my father grew up in a very proper and ambitious home. My grandmother was a first-grade school teacher who did NOT approve of homeschooling. She worried about us constantly but mostly kept quiet about it. My grandfather ran a textile mill that went out of business shortly after a supporting company burned down. He died from cancer a short time after that. I have one paternal aunt who is seven years older than my father.

My aunt and cousins always knew I was being forced into a disadvantage. I've been described as "young, impressionable, socially immature, and inexperienced," but they had no idea the extremism that took place until I began to speak out about it.

We went to my grandmother's house every Sunday after church, where we had polite conversation over afternoon tea. We never spoke of family turmoil. I think my father swore at the table once and was immediately excused. No one ever uttered the word "cancer" when speaking of my grandfather's death. All I knew about his passing was that my Grandma's sister knew something was terribly wrong that day; when she came to my grandparents' home, she found that they had left the house without making the bed. My father got involved in drugs and alcohol for a while (he's now been sober for 32 years), but no one ever spoke of that either. My father would talk about it when sharing his testimony and warning us of the dangers of addiction, but the rest of the family seemed to have erased that part from the family history.

My mother's childhood was probably as opposite to my father's as you can get. My Gramma came from a family of 11 kids, one of whom was a cousin and also half-brother, born to her father and her 14-year-old aunt. The incestual rape that took place in her home was common knowledge in our family, as if it was a natural part of childhood. Gramma was the youngest. She grew to have an obsession with animals after she was told that Flicka, the calf, was her very own pet. However, Flicka was later served for dinner. Gramma has had a house full of animals for as long as I can remember. She is currently 94 and has given my dog, Lady, a home while I moved to multiple pet-free apartments for my husband's school. We're now living in a space where I can have Lady again, but she's Gramma's, til death do they part. Gramma doesn't actually "own" any cats, but shamelessly steals cats from the neighbors. That's not an exaggeration; it's a whole thing and she is unstoppable. I learned the hard way that if Gramma asks you to bury a dead cat, make sure the cat wasn't stolen first.

My grandfather... Well, we may have stumbled on the root cause of cult joining. This is one of those stories I'm not sure how to begin. However, I'm happy to live by the rule "Write drunk, edit sober," as I order another martini and type away in the brick-walled nook of my favorite restaurant where my pasta always comes with broccoli because when my friend Rachael tends bar she makes sure I'm eating vegetables. That'll happen when your favorite bartender is also one of the super moms in your playgroup. So, I'm sure that the version you're reading is far less triggering than my first draft.

As I sat in therapy talking about my wonderful relationship with my grandfather, my therapist asked if I knew what "grooming" was. I told her that I didn't. I'd only ever heard of grooming as a positive experience for pets. When she explained it to me, I left therapy and couldn't function at all for about two days.

I always thought that my grandpa was my biggest fan. He spoiled me rotten. He'd gotten me a massive collection of porcelain dolls that I adored. When we went out to lunch with him every Monday, I always picked the venue. This drove Gramma bananas, but, having been the only grandchild for five years, I was "the favorite," and I got to do whatever I wanted. Even when I eventually had a younger cousin, they were never allowed to be near Grandpa without my aunt or uncle, which I found extremely strange, seeing as he was so kind to me. I always got to watch all the episodes of Little House On The Prairie that I wanted when we would lie in his bed together. This all simply meant that I got to remain the favorite for longer. My sister wasn't born until I was 7 and, by then, I was the alpha grand-child who could do no wrong. I understand now that things were different for my cousins because my aunt and uncle acknowl-edged the dangers that my mother ignored.

My grandparents met at an Army dance. To me, it always sounded like a surreal 1940s courtship that I'm sure was filled with White Christmas-style dance routines. As an adult, I've learned that I come from a lineage of women who got married in order to escape their father's abusive home.

My maternal grandparents' house was chaotic, even when both my mother and uncle were grown. I remember that my aunt spent her first Christmas with our family reading the dictionary; that's how awkward things were. Honestly, I think she was the only one who was uncomfortable with the yelling, since we all thought reading at all was weird. We didn't read, ever. To her credit, she is now a published author, and everyone else is still yelling.

I'm told that was one of the more mellow holidays, seeing as others have involved:

—The turkey not cooking fully because my grandfather had torn off the oven door in a rage before it was cooked.

—Furniture being thrown into the fire because no one had a yule log.

—My grandfather causing a usual scene in a department store as he pulled a fully decorated tree off the display in order to bargain for it. His reasoning was, "It's Christmas Eve, no one else is going to buy it."

—Playing "Dog-shit Easter hunt" because Gramma didn't feel like hiding eggs in the yard. About a week before Easter, she would stop cleaning up after the dogs, so there would be enough for everyone. Actually, it's going to upset my mother if I call it that. So, I apologize... "Dog-shit Resurrection Day hunt."

On a recent visit to Gramma's house, I noticed that there are two bolt locks inside my mother's childhood bedroom door. By now, my mom is used to my I'm-gonna-need-to-know-why face. So, she rolled her eyes and told me about the locks: "Oh, you knew those were there! I needed two because Grandpa broke the first one, and the second he was able to shake open if you jiggled the door enough." She went on to tell me how she had picked this bedroom because of the way the door faced a close wall and she could sit against the wall with her feet on the door, in case the locks failed. If you follow me on Instagram you can actually watch this conversation happen in real time.

At first, I was confused about why my mother wanted the room with the locks, since her brother was the one who was beaten. I later learned that she started needing the locks when she was 11 because my grandfather would come into her room while she was asleep, undo her nightgown, and she would wake up half naked. Evidently, Gramma learned that this was happening and my grandfather told her he needed to check that my mother was "developing properly," which seemed to be enough of an explanation to hush Gramma. He also told Gramma that he forced my mother to lather him in the shower and watch/assist with his bathroom routine, so she "wouldn't be curious about the neighbor boys and get into trouble."

I'm sure you see how ridiculously transparent his lies were but we all believe what we want to believe. I don't think anyone wants to believe that their husband who openly beats their son is also molesting their daughter. Since my grandfather "only acted that way when he was drunk," it also became easier to blame the alcohol than the person.

I've been talking to Gramma about my writing. She often mentions that she never would have put up with the stupid rules we had to live with, like having to ask her husband what she could wear and when she could leave the house, and wonders what drove my mother to want to live like that. I finally asked Gramma if she really didn't see how poorly my grandfather treated her. Did she not see that being abused is all my mother had ever known?

Gramma is my favorite person to interview because you can never predict her answers. She told me, "Wellll, yeah, 'The Man' (which was what the entire town called my grandfather) was an asshole but I always wore whatever I wanted!" It's fascinating to sit and watch her own words sink in. As she reflected, she told me about a time early in their marriage when she was pregnant with my uncle. She'd gone to church and when she came home, my grandfather hit her across her face for having left the house without telling him. She said that at that point, she was stuck. She couldn't go back to her parents' abusive home and she couldn't have a kid on her own. So, she convinced herself that each time was the last time, and she stayed.

For generations, my family has been so focused on the small amounts of grace granted to them by their abusers that they lost sight of how utterly tyrannical their relationships actually were.

As I was getting my girls ready to go trick-or-treating last Halloween, my mother said, "It's going to be really nice that we finally get to have some good memories of Halloween." I asked if she meant because, as a kid, she and my father always had us hide in their bedroom after ordering Domino's pizza at 3 p.m. and then sit in the dark until the trick-or-treating stopped. She said, "No," and laughed, as if those memories weren't even on the radar for strange behaviors. I asked the same question I always ask when my mother casually mentions something that will undoubtedly lead to the uncovering of yet more childhood trauma: "What did you mean, Ma?"

She said she meant that my grandpa usually beat my uncle, while my mother was favored and unhit. I'm not sure if "unhit" is a word, but I feel like I don't need to define it. But, on Halloween, she wanted to wear a princess dress and my grandfather had gotten her a cowboy costume. She refused to wear the costume and was beaten.

I was surprised to hear this story, not because I didn't think grandpa was abusive, but because I didn't think he beat my mother - ever. Grandpa being abusive was never something I witnessed; but, unlike my paternal grandfather's unspoken cancer history, everyone in my family pretty much accepted my maternal grandfather's abuse as a thing that just happened.

Several years ago, I was on a conference call with my mom, Gramma, uncle, aunt, and cousins. This was something we used to do almost daily before people stopped speaking to each other. (I was the first to be cut out. I had been tolerated after my first husband left and then finally cut on the day I announced I was having twins with my current husband). But, during this call, my uncle was talking about the time grandpa had beat him on the living room floor and then actually felt remorse when he thought he had broken my uncle's toe. Gramma interrupted - I don't know if she has ever not done so - to say, "No, no! That's not what happened. Your father never beat you on the living room floor. He always made sure to beat you on the couch because it was soft."

You hear it, right?

But what is it that actually draws a person to a cult in the first place? From what I understand, it's a series of small yet meaningful events. Although my mother is the one who led our family into fundamentalism, my father became all encompassed.

As her yearbooks will tell you, my mother was a smart kid. Top three in her class, actually. She is pretty and a people pleaser to the extreme. She often says her goal in life is "to avoid being yelled at at all costs". Honestly, that used to be my goal, too, until I realized that most of the people doing the yelling are assholes, so their words are meaningless.

Aside from Halloween and when he was drunk, my mother got nearly everything she wanted from my grandfather's grooming behaviors, to the point at which my uncle suffered neglect for it. Throughout her childhood and teenage years, my mother was also molested by her grandfather, extended family members, and parents of her friends; in her eyes, it normalized many of my grandfather's actions and seemed to erase what he had done, since his actions were interspersed with grooming affection.

None of these people were part of ATI, so I fully understand that evil comes from many different places, no matter the upbringing. However, that does not make ATI's form of abuse any less evil.

I spent a large portion of my childhood with my maternal grandparents. My mom had a wedding video business and my grandfather bought her all of the highest tech equipment, which included a camcorder she could support with just one shoulder. She and my grandfather would either film the weddings together or she would work with another friend (who was later convicted of pedophelia) and I would spend the day with my grandparents.

This friend was a teacher full-time, and an avid follower of Bill Gothard. He attended the Basic and Advanced multiple times, although he could not be accepted into ATI due to a previous marriage and divorce.

I remember my parents talking about attending some of Bill Gothard's first seminars with this particular pedophile (we know several from the various cults we've been in), who "famously" proclaimed "I am not a Sodomite!" during a lesson on sexual transgressions which had evidently confused him in the past.

I grew up knowing this man fairly well. Every Monday night when we would go to Gramma's house, Gramma, my mom, and I would all write him letters while he was in prison. I was about 13. I thought it was strange that he would be kept in prison so long for a crime he didn't commit. But then again, that happens all too often, so I trusted my family and kept writing to him. We sent family photos and he would write back about how beautiful we were, saying he wished he had been lucky enough to have been my father. One day, he did send us a full written confession with details of how he had molested a 6 year old disabled student in his classroom. I couldn't understand why, even then, my family didn't stop writing to him. I guess it's the same reason so many of us stay in damaging relationships. As unspeakable as it may be, we are terrified of the unknown, terrified to allow the narrative of someone we trusted to be entirely rewritten. We crave the stability of what we know to the point of relinquishing our own boundaries.

When she was 19, my mother came home on a break from college. In an effort to build a normal family life, she wanted to start making meals, but discovered there was no food in the house, nor money for food because my grandfather had spent everything on alcohol.

She tells me she went to visit the pastor of the church she had attended as a child, but had since been absent after Gramma refused to return when they asked her to wash their curtains. My mother hoped the pastor and his wife would be able to offer some guidance and possibly a bit of food.

She told them of her plans to move out and finally be free of a toxic home but that pastor told her to stay. He told her that, no matter what, my grandfather was her authority and she belonged at home until she was under the authority of her husband. The couple then invited her to attend The Basic Seminar with them the following day. That seminar promised her peace. Since she had never found a possibility of such before, she bought in completely.

By Thursday, she had fallen under Bill's hypnotic spell. She bought into his propaganda of having to "yield her rights" to God, meaning she didn't deserve a home with nutritious food, control over her own body, or anything we consider a basic human right. If God allowed her to have these things, it was merely a bonus. She didn't open the Peter Frampton LIVE record she'd gotten for Christmas because she had been convinced that all the turmoil in her life had been caused by rock music. She accepted my grandfather as her full authority until she transferred that power to my father six years later.

My parents had known of each other's existence for most of their lives due to growing up one street apart, which was super convenient for me when visiting grandparents. Although my mom claims to remember my father coming over to watch Mr. Rogers' Neighborhood with my uncle, Gramma will tell you that their first "real" interaction was at Caldor's department store in 1982. My mom says that Gramma rushed her out of the store because, "that guy was going to ask you out." Eight weeks later, my parents were engaged. They married in June of 1983, 10 days before my mother turned 26.

I don't know much about the years between their marriage and my birth. I do know that my paternal grandma would always say she had never seen anyone so enamored with a baby as my mother was with me. She lived for me. She had spent her entire life wanting me and she was not about to let go. After a decade or so of attending Bill Gothard's seminars, my mother discovered that homeschooling was an option she had never considered. Not only could she keep me by her side at all times, but she could do so under the direction of the organization that had given her the first feeling of security she'd felt after a childhood of bracing her feet against her bedroom door.

At first I was just regular homeschooled with Hooked On Phonics and whatever Comprehensive Curriculum the price club had that lined up with the average grade for my age. We mostly used those for math and history. About half of the science pages had to be torn out though since they taught evolution. Even though we weren't in ATI in those early years, a lot of the beliefs were already there from all those seminars. The church we had been attending was pastored by one of ATI's founding families, so most of the church was "called by God" to join as well.

Joining ATI is an extensive process, which many fail due to the strict, fundamental, and patriarchal demands. When I dug up the application recently, I had to stop reading to ask my mother what it was about the application that made her think she was not, in fact, joining a cult. She said "Bill told us it wasn't a cult".

To save you the horror of looking it up, here are a few red flags on the application:

—"List all unmarried family members." That's the first line. ATI does not have a cut-off age for being under the authority of one's parents. So, rather than list all minors, technically an ATI "student" could be in their 40s.

—Another question is "Are any of your children resistant to joining ATI?" and you are to explain why in a separate letter. Further down in the application, it states, "Some of the most effective young people in ATI were originally enrolled by their parents against their own wishes. They are now grateful for their parents' leadership in taking this step. Please have any of your children age fourteen or older send a letter to the Admissions Department explaining how HE feels about being in ATI. Please let us know if you have any children who are resistant to the program, and please share the reasons."

—"Is there anyone living in your home who is not part of your immediate family?" This seems like an extremely odd question but I'm now realizing that very few, if any, families hosted foster children or exchange students. You can't legally homeschool a child who isn't yours. On the next page it states, "Because of the unique design of ATI, extra pressures occur when unrelated individuals are in the home. Thus, it is necessary to maintain a policy that others not live in the home of an ATI family." Translation: Older kids are gonna hook up, your kids are gonna want to go to school and have actual friends, and you can't maintain complete dominance over those who are not your offspring or spouse.

—"Are you committed to harmonious music as explained on page 4 of this form?" Page 4 states: "...rock music (whether secular or Christian), with its repetitious structure, causes the listener to either react or come under the domination of the music and the message being communicated by the musicians." We'll dive much deeper into that one in a bit.

A few other "standards" included in the application process are:

—Only heterosexual, legally married couples are enrolled. Some exceptions can be made for single parents, such as those who have been widowed, are no longer in a marriage due to severe abuse (case-by-case basis), or were already a single (never married) parent at the time of God's conviction in their lives to turn from their sinful ways.

—You may not join ATI if you have been divorced and/or remarried unless you have provided additional documentation on the following: why the previous marriage ended, your current relationship with the Ex, and written consent from the Ex if any of their children will be enrolled. You must also complete a "Rebuilders" course on relationships and the damage you have already done to yourself, your children, and your new spouse.

There are four pages of cult warning signs, but some that jumped out at me are:

—"...ATI leadership and experienced ATI families strongly recommend that you completely remove the television from your home."

—"..[A]bstain from alcohol, tobacco, pornography, gambling, rock music, and immodest clothing. Your commitment to these standards will encourage your children to avoid even the appearance of evil."

—Finally, they want to assure you will adhere to all patriarchal gender roles: "In ATI, the mother fulfills a vital role in the success of her family through the daily implementation of the program. Outside employment would restrict her effectiveness in this function. If you have a home industry or a family business, include an explanation of how you plan to organize your schedule to teach your children."

My mother did have her wedding video business. We were still accepted though, because it was a business she performed with her father and it only took her outside of the home on weekends. She did all of the editing and demos at home. I remember feeling vitally important in the business when I was in charge of Scotch taping childhood photos to the cleanest spot on our living room wall so my mom could film them for seven seconds, then tape, film, and repeat. She gave it up soon after joining because, shockingly, having a business and trying to homeschool two kids is exhausting. My mother gave up her entire livelihood to homeschool us. After she gave up her wedding business, we were really all she had left.

We were always taught that depression was created by lazy people as an excuse to reject the joy of The Lord. Only now, looking back, am I able to see how severe my mother's undiagnosed depression was. People say I quote movies or shows unusually often, but that's because I used to watch a lot of TV. ATI had a two-hour-a-week TV limit, but my mother would have "forbidden movie days" (mostly Disney movies containing magic and premarital prince kissing). I see now that was her only way of escape.

After we've all been quarantined to our homes for months, it's much easier for you to imagine what my entire hidden childhood was like and why my mother could spend a few days in the same pajamas, watching TV with us in her bed. Sometimes, if we were ambitious, we'd move to the couch. At the time, I had thought days like that were fun. Now, I wish I could go back in time and get my mother the help she needed.

In 1997, our family was accepted into ATI and we made our way to our first conference in Knoxville.

At our first conference, I was 9 and my sister was 2. My family went all in. My father worked as an usher and my mother worked the "family viewing room," where parents of children in the process of blanket training hung out. I went to Pre-Excel. The ironic part is that by my parents jumping into these service roles headfirst, they didn't actually spend much time sitting in the sessions, listening to what was happening around them. My parents are often shocked by my stories of what ATI really was, because they were never in the thick of it as I was. The kids got indoctrinated, but parents were there to serve.

And isn't that how they get you? They make you feel needed. They schedule sessions from dawn to dusk, inducing sleep deprivation for a week, demanding you be fully present for whatever it is God has to reveal to you. If you are too tired to make it to a session, that's the Devil trying to keep you from hearing what God brought you here to hear.

You go home exhausted, already missing the friends who have become one-in-spirit with you, convinced that no one back home will understand the level of conviction you've experienced. You isolate yourself, so as not to let this excitement fade, to prevent the Devil from dousing your fire for the Lord.

And, just like that, you're in.

3

Gaslighting 101

"The Battleground between God and Satan is the human mind. Any person who claims to be "'broad-minded'" or "'open-minded'" is totally unaware of spiritual warfare and is an easy target for false presuppositions which sound as if they are completely logical."

—Wisdom Booklet 49

So, you joined a cult. Now what?

What had been abundantly clear to your yielded Spirit in Knoxville often becomes fuzzy and difficult to explain when you're back home and someone asks what ATI is; one look at the curriculum makes it evident that it sure isn't a valid educational system.

Not to worry. The leaders expected this to happen. Every ATI seminar has a book table, a miniature traveling store at which you can purchase tools to aid in your journey to indoctrination. Here, you can find instructional videos on "How to Respond to Criticism," "How to Answer Questions on Legalism," "How to Recognize and Conquer the Addiction of Rock Music" (those three are available together on a single VHS), and "How to Communicate Biblical Truth to a Secular World."

ATI warns you will be ridiculed for being legalistic and "narrow-minded," but that's exactly what you hope to have happen.

Wisdom Booklet 49 explains, "Most people believe that by learning information, we will acquire knowledge. This idea is not true. As we receive information through our physical senses, we must attach it to presuppositions which are in our hearts and minds. If these presuppositions are according to the strait way, we will have Godly knowledge. If they are based on the opinions, conjecture, speculation, and theories of the broad way, we will have worldly knowledge." If you're often told you're closed-minded and prejudiced, you're winning at cult life.

Real school curriculums don't hand out actual tests asking "How do you show love to a homosexual?" or show a video of a man limping and ask "What do you think is causing this man to limp?" (at least from what I hear, since I don't actually know firsthand). Or maybe they do and the answers are "By being a decent human being" and "Differential diagnosis of gout? Back injury? Leg length discrepancy?" I can only speculate.

What I do know is ATI's answers were always intended to point back to their agenda. Their answer was to become a prayer warrior for homosexuals you may have met, so they could be released from the Devil's grasp. ATI is careful to warn you not to become a prayer partner, since prayer partners must be of the same sex if not related, and it would be dangerous to be alone with someone who could lead you into temptation, since sexuality is a choice in ATI's eyes. As far as the man with the limp? He was obviously limping due to the extreme bitterness he was holding onto for years; the stronghold built on ground yielded to Satan was now presenting as a physical ailment. This was in the actual answer key. Of course, mental health problems can emerge as physical conditions, but this was just another one of their slow, manipulative tactics training us to look at others as Spiritually inferior, while aiding our cult member confirmation bias.

The first few Wisdom Booklets are mostly orientation to "How a Fundamental Extremist Thinks" and are perfect for getting you started on your journey to raising a quiver full of isolated, judgmental, and educationally neglected children. The lessons are focused on looking at the world through different eyes, disguised as "Creativity" and "Wisdom."

You'll find example after example on how to determine everything you should know about a person just by looking at them and why it's important that we all dress so people would know, at one glance, we were bodies yielded to the Lord. They tell you a few seemingly normal things, like how to enhance your countenance with beautiful, time-consuming hairstyles, delicate necklaces (no lower than your clavicle), and earrings (if your husband/father permitted it, of course). Makeup is allowed, but only that which has been deemed pleasing to your husband/father. Ok, so far that's not too extreme, especially if your husband is fairly lenient. It was vitally important we keep the young ladies pure for Bill… or rather, their spouse. It was up to us to dress modestly so we were never a temptation to the young men. #ModestIsHottest, after all. If you've joined ATI, you're obviously into purity culture. So, allowing them to control the way you dress seems like a reasonable step. See? They told you this wasn't a cult!

One could argue that everyone should be allowed to dress however they want, and it's never, ever the fault of the girl in a mini skirt if a guy rapes her. ATI is quick to point to convenient verses that, taken out of context, perfectly reveal why God disagrees. 1 Corinthians 8* focuses on whether or not you can eat meat that had been offered to idols (the answer is basically "It doesn't matter, but don't do it just to be a jerk to someone else"). Yet verse 9 is commonly thrown at any girl who dares not safety pin the gaps in her blouse: "But take heed lest by any means this liberty of yours become a stumbling block to them that are weak."

"That liberty of yours" is often said mockingly to the more rebellious among us, in an effort to remind us that our liberty is a right we should have already yielded to God. ATI will often give examples of "liberty" in a negative context, highlighting sinful synonyms such as autonomy, right, and freedom. As individuals, we were expected to yield our liberty/rights/autonomy/freedom to God and accept anything that happened to us from that point on as God's will. I was terrible at grasping this concept and refused to relinquish my autonomy. I paid for that later in my journey.

Contrary to popular belief, not everyone who joins ATI is convinced they need to have a thousand kids. A lot of people join thinking their family is just the size they want. They're done with the diaper stage and ready to move into the school-age phase. Not so fast. I ended up with a sister seven years my junior in the same way many of my friends did; our parents heard the story of The Lost Pearl.

In this story, a young girl is happily playing on the beach, collecting shells. She finds an oyster shell with a strange rock inside of it, so she tosses the rock into the ocean and keeps the shell. She later learns she had been holding a genuine pearl but carelessly threw it away, and will never have the chance to hold that pearl again.

People will tell you "the world is your oyster" but, in ATI, the oyster is your uterus and it's full of pearls, aka unfertilized eggs. Every time you have a period, it's a reminder that you've thrown away yet another one of your irreplaceable pearls.

Now, most quiverfull people will tell you they keep having kids because they want God to control the size of their family. But it goes beyond that. Bill's stated goal closely resembled that of a dictator, in that if ATI families kept their mass production of "perfect" offspring going, while the world leaned further into birth control and abortions, we would eventually be the majority and could essentially take over the world.

Because no one wanted to invite divine punishment upon their family for their willful disobedience, many of the parents went so far as to have their reproductive surgeries reversed. What started as that twinge of joy you get when you smell a baby's head, accompanied by the thought, "Maybe I should have another one," was quickly manipulated into relinquishing any carefully made, logical, and even medically necessary choices to Bill's narrow-minded, glorified agenda.

This type of surgical obedience was celebrated with "The Reversal Choir," made up of all the children born after a surgical undoing. You want to know what ATI moms gossip about? About who put their kid in the reversal choir after claiming that a change of heart is equivalent to reproductive surgery. What a weird thing to cheat at, yet it's something parents would do year after year when they didn't have enough Spiritual hierarchy points for Bill to notice how humbly submissive they were being. You don't join a cult expecting you'll be trying to one-up the undoing of another woman's tubal ligation, but one day you wake up in Knoxville, put on your best maternity denim jumper, and you're in too deep to go back.

You may be familiar with the story of how to boil a frog alive. If you drop a frog into boiling water, it will recognize the danger and jump out; but, if you put it in tepid water and ever so slowly increase the temperature, the frog will adapt to its environment, oblivious of its imminent destruction. That metaphor for a sinful life has been told at every revival service I've attended and I know it's common during speeches, as well.

DID YOU KNOW THAT STORY IS A LIE?!?!

To paraphrase the reptile and amphibian curator at the Museum of Natural History, the analogy is "bullshit." Learning as an adult that the very reason I refused to step one foot into Hot Topic as a teenager was a lie was devastating. How many things had they lied about?

They lied about all of it.

All. Of. It.

You know the line in the Broadway song that goes, "There's a fine, fine line between a fairytale and a lie"? That's what plays in my mind every time I walk past that giant bookshelf of ATI's literature. As I flip through the Wisdom Booklets, I can see the pure manipulation in every section. As a child, though, I bought every last word of it. Now, I need to read in small increments because the weight of the betrayal is too heavy to handle in binge sessions. Each time I read an uncited "fact," followed by the warning, "Any other conclusion is willful rejection of this obvious truth," it's another reminder that I was actively robbed of a legitimate education or any form of critical-thinking development.

Deciding which of their brainwashing lies to highlight for you is overwhelming. For years, I've been trying to pull passages for this book to finally get people to believe me when I say I was in a cult and wasn't just a prick-kicking teenager. You might need some context for that one. Acts 9:5-6: "And he said, Who art thou, Lord? And the Lord said, I am Jesus whom thou persecutest: it is hard for thee to kick against the pricks. And he trembling and astonished said, Lord, what wilt thou have me to do? And the Lord said unto him, Arise, and go into the city, and it shall be told thee what thou must do." In fundie, "prick-kicking" means "obstinate," as an ox who is fighting his plow.

Short of letting you read my entire old curriculum (which I will totally do if you want to come over), there's no way to relay just how far they went to keep us fully reliant on them, whilst turning us against anyone outside the cult. I eventually decided to pick some Wisdom Booklets at random and see if I could find a good example of how they slowly boil the frogs alive, but with an accurate metaphor. My random selection proved quite effective. I started sticking Post-its to each page containing something either legalistic, misogynistic, hateful, racist, homo/transphobic, or medically/historically/scientifically false. I'm out of Post-its.

To start, I randomly pulled Wisdom Booklet 49, which most ATI families wouldn't get to for several years. When I showed a few fellow ATI-alumni what I'd re-discovered, their responses were all the same: Bill knew that by the later Wisdom Booklets, he could say whatever he wanted and we would all take it for actual gospel.

Bill has been gaslighting people in this way from the very beginning of The Basic Seminar. New attendees may enroll in the six-day seminar on Monday or Tuesday but, from Wednesday through Saturday, only those who have attended the first two nights may enter. Each night, you're told that something in your life will come up that will be "more important" than finishing the full seminar. Someone close to you will tell you the things you're learning are meant to brainwash you. Bill correctly predicts these events because, well, it's accurate. You ARE being indoctrinated into a cult, and pretty much anyone who gives a fuck about you will try to stop you from diving any deeper.

You're warned that these distractions are sent from the devil himself. This warning not only gets you to return to the seminar each night, but simultaneously makes everyone who's lonely, rejected by The World, and reliant on the like-minded Gothardites all head toward Wisdom Booklet 49's blatant agenda of Bill's followers becoming the majority.

Before you scoff, thinking something so ridiculous would ever happen, consider the administrations the U.S. seems to adore. I dove into ATI's teachings on the evils of democracy, which evidently have been the bane of American evangelical existence since the very beginning. In my ATI history assignment I learned: "In a democracy such as the U.S. has become, this balance is destroyed by the concern for majority rule and minority rights. It seems that Americans today prefer representatives who are responsive to public opinion rather than men of character who will vote as their consciences dictate." It's yet to be confirmed, but I'd be willing to fall into gambling's pit of temptation and bet you I know someone who was at the insurrection.

The lesson goes on to outline exactly who should be in political office: "1. Able men - ...[A] capable man who has proved himself successful in his leadership role in his family and in his business profession [Bill LOVED former VP, Mike Pence for these reasons]... not a professional politician. 2. Fear God - He must be under God's authority in order to exercise authority properly... 3. Men of Truth - He does not seek to deceive, either by what he says or does. 4. Hating Covetousness - He must be blameless and above all reproach..."

Now, many of those things are attractive attributes of a political candidate, which is exactly why gaslighting works as well as it does. Why wouldn't we want an elected official to be one of us, to be honest and accountable? It's the other misogynistic characteristics that cause the problems. There's no way you've gotten this far into this book without having at least one foot in the forward-thinking pool, so I'm sure you noticed the multiple times the male pronoun is used in this job requirement. This is not for brevity by any stretch of the imagination, like when parenting books switch randomly between he and she. We were strictly forbidden from voting for a woman, no matter where she stood on the issues. While universally annoying on principle, it was highly entertaining to watch the fundies squirm all the way to the polls when Palin ran for Vice President.

After my historical deep dive, I began reviewing one of the many lessons "proving" that evolution is impossible. Gaslighting cult leaders don't get where they are by not being convincing; they know that by peppering in true scientific statements, it makes the lies much more difficult to distinguish.

In such overwhelming misinformation, it's impossible for me to figure out just how much I don't know or what I have to relearn completely. Sometimes, I'll get intensely invested in my kids' educational shows and my husband will record me in awe, as I learn about the evolution of bananas or actively learn about dinosaurs, while reading the kids a bedtime story.

On one hand, this is helpful in being able to recognize when my homeschool is showing. On the other hand, this makes me feel as if I will always be inferior to those around me. I've fought my way through the patriarchy of submissive women who remain silent unless they've cleared their words with their husband first. Yet, imposter syndrome still runs free in my brain whenever I make the argument that I should be seen as my husband's—or any educated person's—equal, when I only learned last year that you can't grow a banana from a banana and that dinosaurs could have seen rainbows.

The more life changes you make as you dive deeper, the more people will start to notice and ask questions. Sometimes, people don't really know what to ask, but they know something is off. We had a variety of scripted answers. One of the more popular ones came from the portion of the apprenticeship newsletter titled "Questions for Mr. Gothard." An anonymous student wrote in to ask, "How can I explain the ATI program to those who do not understand?" This was Bill's response:

First, it is important to see the bigger picture. Three men were laying bricks. When the first worker was asked what he was doing, he replied, "I'm making a living." The second worker answered, "I'm building a wall," but the third worker explained, "I am constructing a great cathedral." Similarly, you have a vital part in constructing one of the most important ministries of our time. It is unheard of to have leaders of cities, states, and nations ask students for counsel and assistance in working with their schools, businesses, government agencies, families, and troubled youths, and yet this is what is happening today.

Second, discern the relationship you have with the questioner. A relative would deserve a more detailed answer than a casual acquaintance. A friend might be more open to your reasons for choosing a non-traditional approach than an educator, and someone with the spiritual gift of exhortation will probably be more interested in what you have to say than one with the gift of teaching.

Third, make sure that your plan of study consists of skills, courses, and ministry opportunities that are in line with your spiritual gift, life calling, and the Great Commission. (Refer to the chart on 'Essentials for Success in Life.')

Based on the above, your comprehensive answer could be, "I am involved in a ministry that is working with leaders around the world to strengthen families through Biblical principles and character training."

If your questioners express interest, consider the possibility of enlisting them as prayer partners, and keep in touch with them. Most questioners simply want you to be a happy, intelligent, and productive citizen. They will usually become as excited as you are about what you are doing.

At the time, I thought that was a brilliant answer because I'd been groomed to believe that The World was never going to understand and the ultimate goal was to get people to stop asking questions, so they don't call Child Protective Services on your parents. You can see he points out that, since educators will have more questions, we were to avoid actual teachers at all costs.

I'm begging you, pay attention to these kinds of wordy but extremely vague answers when you're talking with a homeschool family. This past year has been anything but normal and there's a larger number of families homeschooling than ever before, but they'll go back to school after the pandemic is over. They aren't the ones I'm talking about. I'm talking about the ones who are willingly homeschooling. In some cases, it's exactly what the child needs most and is the very best option for that child. I'm talking about the ones who were isolated before COVID hit, who will stay that way long after it's safe.

I WISH people had dug deeper when I gave them those answers. When I was a kid, I didn't know I needed an adult to rescue me. I wish they had recognized that my family's parroted explanations were nothing but brainwashed shit. I knew I was weird, but that was as far as it went; I had no idea how bad it was until I was able to stand on the outside looking in.

I'm not sure what it's going to take or how many children will be abused before people see that the lack of a valid education is only scratching the surface of reasons why we need adults to notice and speak up. I've personally watched as known rapists and pedophiles roam freely, and were welcomed into the church and our homes. Now that the TLC star's crimes are coming to light, I pray people will start to see how unfazed we all are. This was our normal. This is what we've been silently screaming about our entire lives, and nobody paid any attention. We aren't just kids who were jealous that we didn't get to be on the town's soccer team. We were kids and we were trapped.

You may have seen the post an anonymous ATI student shared on social media of Bill's lesson: "Why did God let a 4-year-old boy be molested by a 15-year-old neighbor?" This 12-point ATI teaching is an example of the stuff that isn't shown to you until you're in too deep to call out what's right or wrong anymore. This lesson references Deuteronomy 21:23, 24- a verse that does not exist. But we were in so deep, and verses were thrown at us so rapidly, rarely did we have time or bravery to fact-check what Bill was teaching...

1 - To teach him his responsibility to cry out to God for help.
   If the boy did not scream for help, he must confess his portion of guilt that he carries by not telling anyone the moment it happened.

2 - To motivate him to dedicate his body to God.
   If he had yielded his body to God, the neighbor would have been raping "God's body" instead of the boy's.

3 - To give him a "moral vaccination" against future temptations.
   He may now be immune to the sinful, sensual desires that others face.

4 - To transform aroused desires to spiritual power.
If molestation has awakened sexual energy, this should be redirected into "Spiritual power."

5 - To motivate him to write God's law on his heart.
The memories need to be repressed with memorizing Scripture.

6 - To concentrate on God's hatred of sodemy.
Really anything they can use to exploit hate on the LGBTQ+ community, they'll use.

7 - To confirm the importance of avoiding evil companions.
Proverbs says "[A] companion of fools shall be destroyed." Taken out of context, this easily shows that the boy had it coming.

8 - To learn how to discern evil companions.
"Your son should now have a natural resistance to anyone who has impure motives."

9 - To work out justice and mercy.
"Once the full facts are known and repented of, mercy may be extended." When this happened within ATI, the offender would be brought to the church, not the police. We were always threatened by the idea that going to the police might expose us as homeschoolers and get us investigated. If the offense was too severe for the church, offenders were sent to the IFB versions of rehab, such as "Reformers Unanimous."

10 - To help parents understand the basis of "genius."
Ready for this one? It's what we'd throw at people when they dug too deep into our lack of socialization. "In a study by the Smithsonian Institute, 40 men considered geniuses were studied in order to find common denominators, ...[the top three were] 1. Parents protected them from contact with other children. 2. They were continually around caring adults who taught them what they knew. 3. They were taught how to creatively solve problems. Based on this, your son should not have been with the other boy, but rather with the adults, so he could learn from

them." Because that's what every parent of a child who experienced unspeakable trauma needs to be told—that it was their fault. That should be great for healing.

11 - To see the need for a daily schedule for the best use of time.
"Free time" was seen as an invitation for sin. Once again, the parents are blamed for not having a strict schedule for the child to follow so he would not have had time to get molested.

12 - To remind the father to pray a daily hedge of protection.
They saved the most obvious reason this was allowed to happen for last. It's because the father failed to "[A]sk God to rebuke the principality over the family in the name and through the blood of the Lord Jesus Christ."

Thousands of you who saw this online were in pure shock. Us Exers? It was validating to see the world become angry and finally acknowledge that we weren't exaggerating and making up excuses we could use to whine about in therapy or blame our parents for our ill-prepared journey through life. This was normal for us. I used to sit at headquarters in the rape confession circles and think, "How did we get here?" No loving parent reads that lesson and thinks, "THAT is what I want for my kids! Sign me up!"

They can't show you this level of horror until you've been compliant in working your way into full submission. If family and friends started to ridicule or step in, that was a sign you were right where ATI wanted you. If you weren't experiencing pushback or turmoil, then you weren't important enough for Satan to stop. Having that strife pull you away from those who were close to you only solidified your allegiance to other cult members who really understood the Lord's calling for their lives.

Many of us Exers not only live with the trauma that came from the oppression of these lies, but also with the guilt that we played a part in spreading the destructive brainwashing. We were taught that we were the superior race and to vote and act with that in mind.

An Exer about half a generation before me wrote one of our most famous table books, "I Kissed Dating Goodbye," and then later disavowed the book and stopped its publication because he saw the damage his teachings were doing. The world needs more people who are willing to admit that everything they stood for at one time was a mistake, even if that means relearning everything you once held to be true. As more and more of us are finding our way out and finally confronting our parents about the damage ATI has done, the more parents I am seeing admitting they were wrong. That they didn't do it on purpose. Cults don't thrive without blind followers and, when you're searching for guidance, you're going to grab the first one that promises to show you the way.

This does not mean our parents should not be held accountable. Quite the opposite. They put us in danger and robbed us of our education. They hurt us in the name of God. I know parents who enrolled because they only had daughters; in their minds, it didn't matter if those girls were prepared for anything but marriage and motherhood, so a diploma seemed useless. Some joined as an escape from a different past. I can say with confidence that not one family was there because of genuine love that wasn't outweighed by fear.

Sure, the world IS a scary place, but hiding isn't going to fix it. In an attempt to save us from The World, we were pulled deeper into a danger hidden in plain sight. I thrive on close friendships and keeping people out of danger, so I tried to pull as many with me as I could. How many kids am I guilty of hurting? I taught those lessons over and over. I had learned ATI's basics of manipulation by pairing every negative correction with 10 praises, making the person much more willing to please you if they think you already like them that much. I don't know how many people I've hurt by my past beliefs, but I know the number isn't zero.

I will never be able to rectify the damage I've done. This book will not be able to undo any trauma I've caused, but it is the next step towards healing.

*When I was writing this, I was about to ask my husband to read through 1 Cor. 8 to see if he agreed with my summary, even though I've never consulted him on my writing. Do you see? Those beliefs of women being inferior Biblical interpreters to men, to an atheist, nonetheless, are so deeply ingrained. Those tiny ghosts of moments appear out of nowhere to haunt me. And yes, I am unequally yoked. Thank you for noticing.

4

But Look At How Well You Turned Out!

"In the same way that an artist or a poet expresses his innermost values and thoughts on canvas or paper, God expresses Himself through that which He has created and desires to create in me. His ultimate goal is that I become His living epistle, known and read by all men"

—Basic Seminar Follow-up Course: Self-Acceptance

I did not choose my origin, nor my upbringing. None of us did. That being said, I am extremely fortunate to have had the ability to choose my outcome. My systemic privileges propelled much of my escape, and I acknowledge that my situation was far less severe than that of many others. Leaving a cult is hard, but I'm grateful I was able to do so primarily by choice, without the risk of physical danger.

Had it not been for my insatiable need to captivate an audience, I would have unquestionably led a life that would soon not matter after my dozens of children were raised and my husband's work was done. I would have lived a role of support for a man's dream, with my own dream having only been to see him succeed.

I'm sure it's an attempt to make me feel better when people who hear my story say, "But look at how well you turned out!" That is quite possibly the most infuriating and dismissive statement I hear. Yes, I am extremely proud of the person I have become and the life I am living. But none of that just... happened. If I just turned out this way, my sister and I would not be the polar opposite women we are.

Situations happened that were out of my control. The ways I responded took massive amounts of extremely painful trial and error as I attempted to navigate my way through a world for which I was never prepared but where I was determined to remain. When someone tells me, "Look at how well you turned out," they don't realize how many regrettable years I spent being a terrible person doing what I thought God wanted. I thought helping the environment was going against God's plan to destroy the earth. ATI warned us often of the evil deception of environmentalism. Anyone who celebrated Earth Day was put on my Anti-Christ suspect list.

This is an actual conversation I had:

My neighbor:"Hey, your parents forgot to put out their recycling this week."

Me: "Nah, they are just trying to do their part to make the rapture happen sooner."

I was that person who told LGBTQ+ couples I loved them as people but could never approve of the sin they were embracing. I was taught to be hateful. I have two incredible sisters-in-law who are trans. It breaks my heart to know I wasn't taught to hate a life path they chose, I was taught to hate them. The Wisdom Books are filled with examples of families who have been blessed after refusing to serve or house homosexuals. There were examples sprinkled throughout the curriculum on how to encourage those who "rejected God's design for them" to wear more gender-conforming clothes and accept themselves for who they really were. In reality, we were the ones rejecting them for who they are.

A question on one of my old tests asked us to explain the proper way to show love to a "sodomite." (The answer was "not love them, and don't use the word 'sodomite'.") I refused to learn another language because I thought if people wanted to live in America, they could learn to speak English. (I deeply regret that phase of my life and the time lost that I could have spent learning another language, which has zero downsides.) I was taught there are different languages because of God's anger over the tower of Babel and fully believed it was God's Will to keep us all separate, that God put us in each country for a reason and we should remain there.

I'm shaking just typing that. That person is a part of me I wish I could erase. I wish I could undo the racist, violently cruel things I said when I wanted to fit in and no one told me I was wrong. I wish my evangelical extremism hadn't set me up to feel superior to those I saved from an overdose. I wish I had done so much more research before supporting organizations that fuel hatred and damage lives.

I'm deeply sorry for being the unforgivable person I turned out to be several years ago. I could have done so much more for the people around me and for the world, but, instead, I took part in the firmly rooted political beliefs of my evangelical parents, and I regret my first three presidential votes. I turned out to be an uninformed climate change denier who didn't care about what was going to happen, as long as it didn't happen in my suburban housewife lifetime. My diaries from the early 2000's are filled with words written by someone I wish I never was. I'm so, so sorry. I did not turn out well at all.

After a great deal of work, I'm a vastly different person now, but I know I can be better. I still make mistakes, often; I'm grateful for anti-racist friends who guide me to a more loving existence. I get to decide how I turn out. And, let's face it, Homeschool Heather was an asshole.

Fortunately, I'm told by those who have known me since I first left ATI that I've left "Homeschool Heather" far in the past. I hope they're right. The thing is, even though I'm no longer ashamed of the fact that I have nipples, vote for women if they earn it, have visible tattoos, and know that Black Lives Matter is not an invalidation of other lives, I do not exaggerate when I say I face an erroneous belief from my past almost daily, a belief I don't realize exists until it creeps into my knee-jerk-reaction responses. For example, if I'm at work and a patient's family member says, "She can't speak and hasn't been out in over a week" (pre-pandemic), I instantly want to destroy that family member for silencing my patient and holding them prisoner; but then I realize the patient simply has a sore throat and malaise, and their family member is offering support. If you've seen the video in which I first learn dinosaurs and humans didn't coexist, you've had a small glimpse of what it's like walking though my life. Every day is a relearning surprise.

The way I live my life now is massively intentional. Using the word "Overcoming" rather than "Escaping" in this book's original title was a conscious choice, deciding to see my actions as a result of my way of thinking. The first time I heard Kimmy Schmidt say, "Escaping is not the same as making it," I knew I hadn't escaped a cult. I didn't escape the person I was on the path to become; I am still in the process of overcoming her. I don't know if my knee-jerk, cult-ingrained reactions will ever fade. I do know that as long as I can recognize them, I can overcome them, and let my patient's family tell me about their flu-like symptoms without having the urge to destroy anyone.

* * *

If you've never been to therapy, I highly recommend it. Maybe you're like me and spent a lifetime being convinced therapy is a direct line to the devil, though I'm pretty sure the devil liked me a lot more before I learned to stop hating entire groups of people.

I didn't start therapy until after my second suicide attempt and extreme mental breakdown that I may not have survived without my husband and Michelle, the Anne Perkins to my Leslie Knope. I'd spent years being unfairly judgemental of patients who needed treatment for anxiety and depression until I realized the only difference between us was they were brave enough to ask for help. I'd been convinced by my Wisdom Booklets that depression is a sign of hidden sin needing to be confessed, which led to a cycle of even more worthlessness. An early Wisdom Booklet teaches that one of the world's greatest deceptions is trusting psychologists with mental health, instead of turning to the Bible, the only counsel one should ever need. Ironically, my belief in the Bible was a huge driving force in my suicide attempts, but we'll get into that in a bit.

We were told psychologists focus first on your mind, instead of searching for the true root of evil festering in the soul. (In looking back and pouring over my curriculum, I noticed that all forms of mental health professionals are referred to as "psychologists" or "humanistic" in a derogatory fashion.) They will counsel based on situational ethics rather than a devine, unchanging law. Perhaps the most repetitive warning I was given was that psychologists will usually reject the fundamental teachings of ATI chosen by our parents, putting us into great danger in trying to get us out from under the umbrella of authority. There are warnings scattered throughout the Wisdom Booklets that psychologists will do everything from insisting husbands and wives have an equal say to taking the easy-out of blaming a neurotransmitter imbalance for depression, taking all responsibility to reject sinful

thoughts off of us and rely on medication instead. I didn't realize it, but I truly believed every word and had rejected multiple
urgent referrals to see a therapist, for fear they would brainwash
me straight into the pit of Hell.

When I finally found a therapist, it was someone I didn't
love, but I figured they all do the same thing and she was just the
one who was available. While she did help, she liked to spend
most of the session talking about how many degrees she had
and recommended taking Benadryl every night rather than dealing with the root of my nightmares. I also started on meds pre-
scribed by a very kind, older psychiatrist, who would curl over in
his chair with his head in his hand, as if I had broken his brain,
every time I said something I'd learned from ATI as if it were
common knowledge. This didn't do much to debunk the lie that
if I went to therapy, I'd get meds tossed at me and I wouldn't
have to do any work. I stopped seeing that therapist when we
moved to Maine. A few months later, I ended up in an insurance
fraud battle with her for double billing and adding sessions I'd
never had. So, you know, that definitely helped solidify any trust
issues I'd had.

When I started therapy in Maine, I was interviewed first to
determine which therapist was the best fit for me, not simply
assigned to the therapist who had the most openings in their
schedule. I started meeting with Paula. This time around was
an entirely different experience; Paula has changed my life by
teaching me how to do so myself. I still have meds, but therapy
is a LOT of work! Sometimes, I'll leave a session and feel physically exhausted. For years, Paula let me bring the twins with
me because I didn't have a sitter. I found that I'd feel far more
exhausted when I'd go alone, though, because we could get to
deeper issues without the distractions of diaper changes and
breastfeeding, which I discovered I'd been using as a crutch whenever a topic became uncomfortable. They had to stop coming

recently because they understand what's happening—although it's adorable when they demand several different meals and start yelling, "Paula said I have the right to change my mind!"

When I moved away from Southern Maine to "Downeast" Maine, I had to stop my appointments, but Paula was fabulous about it and still emailed and talked on the phone during the transition. A year later, I moved back to Southern Maine and she made room for me in her schedule, even though she was technically full. She and I have similar tastes and we get along beautifully; I feel like if we had met under different circumstances, we would have been friends. But maybe she's just that good at her job, and saying my therapist would be my friend is like when guys think the stripper was actually into them. I'm eternally grateful for everything she's taught me. Without her, there is no way I'd still exist today.

As it turns out, ATI was right about something; my therapist did in fact suggest their teachings were legalistic extremism disguised as the path to ultimate blessings. The first time I brought my box of Wisdom Booklets to therapy, Paula didn't talk for almost the full hour. She flipped through page after page, the silence occasionally broken with gasps, as she turned back pages to reread what couldn't possibly have been part of a serious educational curriculum. When my hour was almost up, she asked, "How is this legal? How do states not tell people that this is by no means a provision for a full education and at least require other materials?! How can they teach against human rights?"

Exactly. But, the thing is, most people have no idea what is taught in homeschool because no one is checking. ATI knows that extended family members will often have questions. In order to keep a cult running smoothly, they provided scripts of responses throughout the first year of Wisdom Booklets with reminders in the newsletters, as you read earlier, to recite if our education came into question.

Most often, people would say ATI was legalistic. They. Are. By definition from Merriam-Webster, legalism is "strict, literal, or excessive conformity to the law or to a religious or moral code; the institutionalized legalism that restricts free choice." However, ATI instructed us to respond that a legalist is someone who believes salvation can be obtained through good works; therefore, since we choose to trust God for salvation, we cannot be a legalist. Yep. That "gotcha!", also used to prove MLMs aren't pyramid schemes because pyramid schemes are illegal, is right there in my curriculum. I never bothered to open the dictionary to confirm any of their definitions; I'm sure they were counting on that when these were written. After all, devout cult members know better than to question the writings of their authorities. That's just Basic stuff (get it?).

As far as being a legal education, unfortunately, it is legal. Some states are more strict than others, but in Connecticut, we weren't required to report to anyone. Some families did, if they wanted their kids to earn a diploma. My parents chose not to tell the state I existed, and my full education was done via ATI from age 9 to "graduation", with one supplement for math. My parents printed me a diploma from a Word document. I don't have a GED—but I'm starting the classes to earn mine as soon as I stop typing and this book goes to print!

* * *

You would think that since I knew little outside of what I could find in a Wisdom Booklet, I would have been in my element whenever I attended an IBLP/ATI conference. But even when I was fully immersed in everything ATI, I still felt like an outcast among the students. I felt I just wasn't spiritual enough to have the joy my friends had. I'd never be as cool as they were, chillin' in whatever quiet place they would make before teaching a children's seminar, memorizing Scripture, and meditating (aka: sleeping) under their bonnets if they were River Brethren (Mennonites couldn't use this trick, as their bonnets were see-through).

My most spiritually comfortable friends would pick flowers and walk through the halls talking to themselves while they were on a date with Jesus, so unbelievably confident that this was the best way to remain pure until marriage. To be fair, it was, but not for the reasons they thought. I've kept or regained contact with many of those girls. As it turns out, a lot of them were just as miserable but had found small coping skills to allow escape for a few seconds at a time. No one yells at you for being too outspoken when you're on a date with Jesus.

I wished I could be just like those girls who gave zero effs about what a guy thought and just go back to reading my Bible, but I liked to hang around the boys. Both because I thought they were handsome, and they got to do way more exciting things than the girls did, like tell the stories and wear pants. The boys got to run outside and play sports while the girls were stuck decorating the team stations and making cute name tags.

There was this one guy who helped decorate our team station for a seminar. I remember feeling bad for him for the sin of male attraction in his life. How shitty was that of me?! I assumed that because a guy fulfilled a "female" role, he must be gay, and saw that as negative. I felt the need to protect him after that; I didn't want anyone else to hate him for what I assumed was true about him. I took on a motherly role when I should have just said, "Hey, nice paper chandelier!" Forming a harsh opinion about a stranger isn't something I stumbled upon on my own. One of the very first assignments in the Wisdom Booklets is to people-watch and find who has hidden sin in their lives. (Hint, they'll be limping and will have made no attempt at countenance enhancement.)

* * *

A popular point people like to bring up is how well-behaved homeschooled kids seem to be. That isn't well-behaved; that is oppressed and abused, and it starts from birth. ATI has a way of exalting abuse while conveniently remaining non-committal enough that they can easily deny such accusations in a lawsuit. Being known as a group of kids who run households and frequently win national spelling bees makes it easy to impress outsiders.

I spoke at length with a fellow homeschool graduate and eldest child about this and I think he said it perfectly: "Homeschoolers' maturity is often fetishized." When he said it, everything clicked in my mind. Of course! Homeschool parents love to brag about their 14 year old taking college courses, but often, that obsession with academics is just as damaging as educational neglect. People idolize our almost standard parentification, especially as the eldest child, and then wonder why we're fascinated by Goosebumps and The Babysitter's Club as adults. It's not that our tastes are juvenile; we are trying to fill an entirely empty gap in our development, grasping at anything we can to feel like we didn't miss out on a part of ourselves we didn't allow to exist, because childish behaviors got us disciplined to the legal limits.

Wisdom Booklet 32 teaches that "Earthly Fathers are to follow the example of our Heavenly Father in the discipline of their children. Lack of correction and discipline will harm a child and ultimately bring shame to the parents..." When I read this, all I can picture is a mother being judged by the childless or the selective memory holders when her child is having an epic meltdown in Target. Discipline isn't about whether or not the child embarrasses the parent. Discipline should be solely focused on the safety of the child, and those around them.

My mother was never the one who spanked me—ok, except for this one time. I was trying to dress my little sister while our mom was in the shower because we had somewhere to be. My sister was screaming at the top of her two-year-old lungs and, as I was leaning over her, my mother suddenly came into the room and hit me, hard, on the butt. I have never been more surprised in my life, and I think I can say the same for my mother. She realized as soon as she hit me that she had made a terrible mistake. That is the only time I remember her hitting me. When I said I was writing this book, my mother asked, "You're going to write about that time I hit you and you didn't deserve it, aren't you?" Ma, you willingly joined a cult. Hitting me once by "mistake" because you thought I was hurting your other kid is nearly meaningless.

All the other times I was hit, it was by my father. He usually used a long wooden spoon. At a conference, he learned that your child shouldn't associate your hand with abuse, so it was best to use an object, such as the Biblically tried-and-true rod. Although my mother didn't cook, we went through a lot of wooden spoons in our house. I remember that, eventually, he gained a preference for the type of wooden spoon he used. He didn't like the long, thin ones much because, although they stung, the pain didn't really last. Those also left a linear mark that was difficult to explain away. Instead, he preferred the ones with the thicker handles and broader, more spatula-type spoons because they didn't break as easily and left marks that looked like we fell. One day when Gramma was over, she took the spoon he kept on his headboard and broke it over her knee. Though he taped it back together, it never regained its power. Around the time I was growing out of being spanked—because eventually it crosses over from child abuse to sexual abuse—he found his favorite spoon. It was wide, short, and had a very smooth handle, so as not to leave splinters in the user's hand. That one was mostly used on my little sister, but not nearly as much as I had experienced. She's a much more compliant human.

My father, following ATI's guidance, was in charge of hitting but also had a full-time job, so sometimes the task was outsourced to my mother. In these cases, I had done something especially disappointing to him and was sentenced to be hit every few hours. Because he was the one in charge of the hitting and didn't believe my mother would hold up her umbrella, he would call home when it was time for me to be hit, in order to confirm my punishment was actually taking place. My mother and I ended up hitting everything in the house that wouldn't break until we found a surface that sounded the most like my prairie-dress-covered butt. The winner was one of the stiff, ugly couch pillows I'd always stared at during home church. When my father would call, my mother would hold the phone close to the pillow, hit it with the spoon as hard as she could, and I would instantly start wailing. Our performance was never questioned. That may have been the thing that bought my undying love for my mother. Even though she did hit me that one time...

ATI had several suggestions on how to break your child's spirit into submission (I'm not exaggerating, that was an actual parenting goal), ranging from assigning meaningless, repetitive tasks, to the favored blanket training. Thankfully, by the time we joined ATI, I was too old to be blanket-trained and my mother despised the concept, so she never blanket-trained my 2-year-old sister.

When we got older and attended the children's seminars during the conferences, we were each given a carpet square as our seat. Even though I had never been formally blanket-trained, I was familiar with the concept and remained fervently planted in the center of my assigned carpet square, as did all the other kids who had grown up in ATI. It was easy to spot "the rebels." They were the ones who would stay on their square, but scoot it around a bit or sit on the back and bend the front up over their knees and then let go, so it made a small "thwap" sound on the auditorium floor, constantly throwing me into a daydream.

What did all these different lines and half circles on the auditorium floor mean? How fast could kids run between the two basketball hoops now folded up to the ceiling? Did kids actually "play" in this room? Did the seats behind the partition really expand to hold the weight of all those parents who cheered for their kids in immodest shorts, who wouldn't so much as recite a verse of memorized Scripture, let alone an entire chapter? Clearly, we had to be sitting in a den of iniquity.

With the next "thwap," I would snap back to reality and realize that, clearly, these rebels were sent by the Devil himself to cause a distraction, so I would miss the message God was trying to give me through my teacher. It never crossed my mind that some kids are just 8 and like to move around.

* * *

Hearing "But look at how well you turned out" holds a specific trigger for me because it's not just something I hear from people as an adult after a gut-wrenching amount of constant remodeling.

ATI exalts those who are grateful for their abuse. I have a 10-step guide from ATI on how to counsel someone who has been sexually assaulted. Steps one through five involve the victim identifying their behaviors and considering why God let this happen. Here are some of the examples given: dressing immodestly/with the intent to defraud men, being with "evil" friends, stepping out from under the umbrella, and being guilty for other sins in their lives. It is recommended that the offender be reported to an authority such as your father or pastor, but ATI often avoids the police and handles sexual assault with counseling sessions or time at the LIT or RU centers.

It isn't until step six that we learn what to say if the assault was not the fault of the victim. This list includes reminding the victim they are now able to experience true joy, knowing they are right with God and that this did not happen as a punishment. The innocent victim will be rewarded with Spiritual strength now that their physical body has been violated. The guide ends with asking the victim the following question: if they could do it all over again, would they choose being mighty in spirit or having never been physically abused?

Ever have those moments when you're with a group of coworkers and someone suddenly makes it awkward by trying to fit in? I do that constantly.

Them: "...Well that's not mutually exclusive."

Me: "What is 'mutually exclusive'?"

Them: "You know, when something has to be either/or."

Me: "Oh gotcha. Like being mighty in Spirit or not sexually abused."

And thus, a casual conversation turns into an emergency session of debunking one of Homeschool Heather's cult myths. When I add things like that in a conversation I never do so to make it weird or extreme, I'm only grabbing a part of what I erroneously knew as a universal teaching.

The person I am now is the most intentional version of myself. I am obviously an incredibly flawed human, but I am a far better human than I had turned out to be when someone else was holding the reins. My mental, emotional, and Spiritual oppression weren't things I could just undo by saying, "Hey, they were wrong. I don't think like that anymore." I left ATI when I was 19 and made the choice to go to medic school and drop out of Bible college when I was 20. I'm now 33 and I am STILL finding beliefs to overcome around every corner.

I've read a ton of personal development books that helped me get past a lot of my own excuses. What bothered me about those books being all the rage in my privileged circles was they only made me focus on myself, and that's not enough. None of them suggested what to do next. After I'd empowered my inner goddess not to take any more shit, then what? What's the point of growing into a strong person if you get stuck in a loop of only focusing on your own success? Personal development is only the first step. Now it's time to fix it for someone else. I can't fix it on my own, I need your help.

I need you to demand that states must have strict homeschool oversight. Even loving parents who want the best for their kids can end up giving them a deficient education. Homeschool kids will slip through the cracks most easily, since they have no adult to go to for help other than the one who is holding them back. Do you know how many homeschooled kids attempt suicide, never learn to read, or are beaten, raped, and exploited by their families every day? No, you don't, because no one knows they are there. I asked one of the data researchers at CRHE if they had a rough idea of how many kids fit into these categories. The truth is it's something no one is able to count. You can't count someone if you don't know they exist.

Many families would prefer homeschool regulations remain as they are now. They tell me they don't need oversight because they are doing everything they should be and then some. Ok, that's great. The problem we're facing is that thousands of families aren't. In order to help homeschool's invisible children, we need responsible homeschool families to take on a small inconvenience in order to ensure that every child is receiving a full, valid education.

Oversight doesn't mean restricting what parents teach their children. Oversight would have still allowed me to use the Wisdom Booklets, or any other religious teaching. Oversight would mean required standards put in place to ensure that each child has the support and resources needed to exercise their right to an education—an education best tailored to the way they learn and what works best for them as an individual, whatever that may be. I want to believe that every single one of you reading this, and every single homeschool parent would gladly accept the potential annoyance of oversight if it would save even one child. Argue all you want, but I know for a fact that oversight would have saved me.

To learn more about what you can do, visit the websites listed in chapter 13.

5

"Homeschool Heather"

"Your life WILL count. It always counts when invested in that which lasts– God's Word and men's souls. Don't look back on life and wish you had done things differently."

— "Verity College of ATI" brochure

In the very, very beginning of my journey through deconstruction I started by writing my story in a blog I titled "Overcoming Homeschool Heather". That was the original title of this book, but I eventually changed it when this evolved from a memoir into a call to action. This is my story, but my situation is not unique. The process of overcoming "Homeschool Heather" is one only I can control. Protecting Homeschooling's Invisible Children, as we are affectionately called by The Coalition for Responsible Home Education, from educational neglect and abuse in the name of love is not something I would ever attempt to overcome alone. It's not about me anymore, so I changed the title.

"Homeschool Heather" started as a comic strip made by some of the girls at the IFB church we attended when I was a teenager. Everyone always knew I was kind of weird, but these girls defined it. I don't think they were bullies, although, as adults, some have taken on that role. Although they had grown up in a fundamentally strict church, they had never experienced a human in my category; so, they made one for me.

Isn't that something so many of us try to do? We want our little world to make sense and, to do so, we insist on fitting everyone into a tidy category, making it convenient for us to decide how to treat them. We do it from the very beginning, when we find out the sex of a baby. If we don't understand the way someone else loves, we scramble to find a category in the LGBTQ+ terms so our brains can maintain this nice, organized image of our world.

Most people wanted me to fit the label of "Amish" and tried to convince me I basically was; to be fair, educationally, we have several similarities. The Amish do not believe in schooling after 8th grade, and they are legally protected under the U.S. Supreme Court's ruling that parental religious beliefs superseded a child's right to an education in 1971's "Wisconsin v. Yoder". The Amish Heritage Foundation was created to help those who were denied an education due to religious extremism, which most people equate with the Amish, but is alarmingly prevalent right down your street. We did have Amish families in ATI but in my mind I was the furthest thing from Amish. I wore clothes with prints and didn't cover my head. I didn't really have a category until "Homeschool Heather- the comic" was passed around during extended altar calls to keep my cohorts awake. As you can see from my online presence as @BacksliddenHarlot, and the back cover, I'm a big fan of claiming the shit people say about me as my own and turning it into something powerful. Had it not been for them, it would have been much more difficult to name my blog and eventually dream up this book's original title.

At the time it hurt but I hear being made fun of as a teenager was one of the more normal experiences in my life. I have the same type of critics now, though in mostly different bodies. People's responses to my writing range from fan-girl to ATI parents who insist they aren't damaging their kids and that I'm just bitter. Fun fact: I wrote that last sentence months ago but had almost that exact comment left on my posts just a few days ago. The "Overcoming" part of the original book title has nothing to do with getting past the teasing. Honestly, it's not about them. It's about me recognizing my hardwired narrowmindedness of oppression and changing the way I respond to the world around me. Friends and family have nervously inquired if they will be spoken of negatively in this book. It's a funny thing to write a book with "abused" in the title while assuring your parents they won't have to sue you for libel (an actual conversation I had with them). This is so much bigger than them. This is bigger than just my individual story, this is about an entire world of hidden abusers right in front of our eyes.

Homeschooling, in and of itself, isn't evil in my mind. The WAY I was homeschooled was. I fully support families who homeschool because it's the best thing for that individual child, and who provide a valid, equal education to the one available in traditional schools. I understand there are many reasons to homeschool outside of being commanded to do so by your cult. I lived in the town next to Sandy Hook. I would have been there if I'd had the keys to the ambulance that day. I listened to it happen over our radios. I heard the death count rise 26 times. No parent should have to wave at the school bus and wonder if their child will be in a massacre. I still respond to calls for the students who were there that day, continually suffering from severe psychological torment. I know several families who decided to homeschool after that, but who went about it in a way that would uplift and support their child rather than hide them. The choice and/or need to homeschool today, through a pandemic, is much different than the one made by parents like mine. Many families, including mine, used the guise of "religious freedom," but that was as much a scapegoat to endanger children as it is when used as a reason against life-saving medical care. I used to think public school was a punishment and, if parents actually loved their children, they would devote their lives to teaching them. It is now abundantly clear to me that I may be incapable of expressing love whilst simultaneously teaching my twins how to write a lower-case "q." Public school was how bad parents got rid of their kids for the day. When I was in trouble, my mom would threaten to call the school bus to pick me up the next day; I would instantly behave. At the time, going to school was the worst thing I could imagine happening to a kid.

When I began writing this book, I never, ever would have thought I would be a homeschool parent. Ugh, I cringe just reading that line as I edit. But here we are, in the extreme circumstance of a poorly handled global pandemic, and I'm trying to take as many deep breaths as I can to get past my own PTSD each time I look at the shelf full of my kids' school. After spending a lifetime trying to disassociate myself from homeschoolers, now most of my friends are homeschooling this year. Knowing this is an entirely different situation doesn't help quell the instant nauseating fight-or-flight response that's triggered every time I see a photo of my friends' learning areas in their homes. I've been one of the extremely fortunate ones who, so far, has only been affected by the pandemic through reliving childhood trauma and waiting for updates from close friends' hospital rooms.

It's surreal to watch as the world tries to navigate the new necessary habits that once held me captive. Until now, I'd seen my homeschool past as something I had overcome and could leave behind, like a bad memory. Now, it means gluing together the shattered pieces of my glass ceiling, hoping it's enough to protect my kids and not scar them with the jagged edges.

My daughter cries during night snuggles and asks why I won't let her go to school like a normal kid. She may never know how deeply that question strikes my soul. I want to make different mistakes as a parent, not the ones I know are likely to traumatize her. Most of what we do is online learning; I wrestle constantly with how to teach a child to read or do math without basing the lesson off the feeding of the five thousand; ATI's entire basis for the Wisdom Booklets is The Sermon on the Mount, recently verified by checking their website. "3000 pages, 54 Wisdom Booklets, 111 verses, 1 Sermon on the mount"

Even just homeschooling kindergarteners is showing me how much was left out of my education. Sight words were never taught because time was better spent memorizing Scripture than word recognition. I think I'd mentioned the concept of sight-reading to my mom once. I probably would have been shunned if I hadn't been 5.

After my parents fell into religious addiction, I no longer fit in anywhere. While we didn't join the cult until I was 9, I was homeschooled from day one, with their steadfast hope that one day the Venn diagram of convenient Biblical misinterpretation and a math curriculum would emerge. At first, I was pretty great academically. I could read by age 4. After watching my mother edit videos of plays she had filmed for the local high school drama program, I could recite entire productions. I learned geography and art because of my father's career as "Huggie the Bear," the balloon-delivering singing telegram. I spent a great deal of my time riding around in his van, stopping just before the assigned address to inflate a bouquet of fuchsia, chartreuse, magenta, jade, tangerine, and cerulean balloons. Thanks to my father's roles, which also included "Spender the Dog," the Easter Bunny, and the mall Santa, my pediatrician was overly impressed at my ability to identify colors during my well visits. (He also chose to ignore his role as a mandatory reporter for the bruises he'd find.)

I was raised in a family of professional clowns. When my aunt was in Clown College, she and my uncle met at a juggling club. They went on to run their own stilt-walking entertainment company and performed at several high-profile events. A few days ago, my kids asked my husband if he could juggle. I was genuinely surprised that he cannot. He correctly told them, "Ask mommy. That sounds like a skill that would have been important in her family." It was so strange to me that someone would grow up not learning such a basic, vital life skill. When I told my cousin about my husband's inability, they were just as baffled.

The first wedding I ever attended was that of a family friend. He was a regionally famous magician who rode a unicycle down the aisle of the theatre they had reserved as their venue, holding a glass slipper in his hand to place on his bride's foot upon his arrival to the stage. Yet people blame Disney for my "unrealistic expectations." When I was 3, I was a flower girl in my aunt and uncle's wedding. At many weddings, the bridal party will hold up their flowers and create an archway for the couple to enter the reception. At their wedding, the bridal party juggled an archway of clubs. While flash mobs may seem extreme to some, I see them as a natural way of keeping up the standard of life being your stage.

I didn't start to notice I was different until I was about 6 or 7. By the time I was 6, I had only been in one class setting: the "Big Sibling" class at the hospital. Due to my sister causing complications in pregnancy, my mother was in the hospital during my class, so we all headed up for a tour of her room, to see what real-life fetal monitoring was like. It was the last time I would ever be the most popular kid in a class of more than one.

When I was 5, a family with a girl four months my senior, Liz, moved in next door to my paternal Grandma. Liz became my magic mirror, my only window to the outside world. Liz lived in the house where all the kids wanted to hang out and she always included me, even if it meant repeatedly explaining to her school friends why she hung out with me. I still remember her old phone number and its exact musical tones from hitting "redial" for a decade. She knew I was weird and even used me as the subject for a paper she had to write. She would learn hymns on her electric guitar so we could play duets after I got a violin. Sleepovers were against the rules, but if she had one, I was allowed to go for the pizza and movie parts and then return to my Grandma's to sleep when the ouija board and PG-13 movies came out.

Liz and I had a typical rebel v. extremist falling out when we were teenagers. She got a tattoo and I had been all-in for ATI at that point. I mourned her choice to defile her body with ink, continuing to isolate myself with only fellow cult members. Thankfully, a few years later, she forgave my extremist, crazy-pants behavior and we became friends again. I love her fearless attitude towards fighting the daily interactions of societal injustices, even if she can't quite put a finger on why they're bad. I shouldn't be surprised; she's done that since she was 5.

My parents now live next door to her old house, where her brothers still live. Last year, I trick-or-treated (with my kids) at her house for the very first time. I sent her a photo of myself weeping in her old driveway. For so many years, I'd watched her leave from that spot to go collect candy while I stayed behind. How much I missed her in that moment was overwhelming. That's normal, right?

Before ATI, I had friends at an Evangelical Baptist church (which is different from an IFB church) who were even kind enough to pretend it was cool to be the one to press the button on my giant nebulizer between Sunday school and the regular service. Most of them got bored of watching the steam come out of my mask and went to do whatever it is popular girls do. But one girl stuck by me. She wore Belle's blue dress every Sunday and shamelessly carried her blankie. She was my hero. I'm happy to say she's still in my life today and has grown into an incredibly strong woman who doesn't conform to what others think she should be.

The other girls were nice—they came to my birthday parties and tried to be my friend—but, a lot of the time, it put them in a tough position. They would ask me to sit with them or offer to sit with me during service, but my father's rules for an hour at church were the same as for sleepovers: "Young ladies belong with their families." As luck—excuse me, providence—would have it, never allowing non-family members to stay in your home is one of the ATI application standards; my father was already well on his way to raising an ATI family before he even started trying. I was only ever allowed to sit next to my friend if her entire family joined us in our row. Sometimes they did, though, and that was very kind.

At one point, I nearly started to fit in when the girls were putting together a song for the church's anniversary. They were writing a parody of "My Girl" about the pastor and I was ALL about it. My brain processes most information in song; my husband thinks it's hilarious to start a line of a song I can rewrite because I'll have to stop and write the entire thing. I helped write the "My Girl" parody, loving every second of the process. I even got to act like I was cool since I knew the song. It was in my favorite movie, "Father of the Bride," so no one had to bring a CD to include me in a conversation about a popular song, like they usually did.

Finally being a part of something that skimmed the surface of normal was my Icarus moment. I had written, practiced and loved every single second of the experience when, one day, my father announced God told him I shouldn't be part of the number. He had heard Bill Gothard's sermons on "The Dangers of Rock Music" and felt convicted that my participation would lead to destruction.

Bill Gothard taught that music was powerful. I'll agree with that, although not to his extremes. Music can enable us to reach emotions that nothing else can describe; I believe we need many types of music as an outlet for things we might otherwise not be able to release or embrace. We were taught to look for several red flags to determine whether music was lifting us up or literally brought to us by Satan himself. A song was deemed sinful if any red flag was recognized. My father was able to use Bill Gothard's red flags to determine that "My Girl" was the devil in an extremely sneaky form.

The first red flag was the dominant beat/rhythm of the song. While all songs have a beat, you'll notice most classic hymns do not have a dominant beat/rhythm. If you don't know how to determine a dominant rhythm, think about the song "Amazing Grace." Could you easily clap along to it? Now, think about "My Girl." Due to the dominant beat of the music, this song had a high likelihood of provoking sensual feelings, another red flag. The song had a beat that allowed natural swaying of the hips. That was a huge point against me.

The worst red flag of all, the song faded out. If there is anything Bill Gothard will not tolerate, it's a song that fades out rather than comes to a conclusive end. I remember my mother used to have a bunch of Steve Green CDs, but once that so-called Christian artist released a modern album with fade-out endings, those CDs had to go during the next Spiritual cleanse. For whatever reason, fade-out songs are purely evil. My father didn't know why he had even allowed me to participate in the first place.

That was the first real fight I remember having with my father. It was the first time I remember screaming back at him, trying with all I had in me to hold onto something that had brought me such joy. Needless to say, I lost. When you're 11, and Tiktok hasn't been invented yet it's pretty easy to get busted when your form of rebellion happens in front of the entire congregation. And people wonder why I involuntarily shout "Amen!" during Footloose.

The celebration came and went. From my place in the audience, I held back tears as I mouthed the words I'd helped to write. I KNEW I wasn't meant to sit in a seat. This had been a chance to embrace my automatic knack for parodies coupled with my blissful inability to tell if a crowd is laughing with me or at me, and I was watching it from my seat. Of every part of my story, that event stirs up the most emotion. Sure, I was the odd-one-out for most of my life, but this wasn't about fitting in. This was about finally being able to reveal everything that came naturally to me to someone other than my mirror. It wouldn't have mattered if I had embarrassed myself that night anyway, since we soon left that church when they bought a drum set.

* * *

A few years later, I started volunteering at the local community hospital as a Candy Striper. I had yet to be devastated by the news that girls can't tell stories, so I was still heavily invested in ATI's lifestyle, with the goal of joining their traveling team. I didn't own pants; since no one wanted to deal with a culture lawsuit, the hospital changed the dress code to "khaki pants or at-least-knee-length skirt." I was the one teenager who wore a massive, floor-length skirt and buttoned my shirts not only all the way up, but also safety-pinned between the button gaps, so no one could see my t-shirt underneath. I was as modest as a teenager could get and owned the eff out of it.

This was the same time the comic of me was circulating around the church. At some point, my church friends met my hospital friends, and soon everyone in my world knew me as "Homeschool Heather." Eventually, the name evolved from one of mockery to one of identity, a way to understand why I acted the way I did and why I often missed the point of punch lines or made normal conversations extremely depressing.

The other Candy Stripers became my closest friends. By the time we were all 17, our group of five had evolved from volunteers to employees. We were all hired to work in "Distribution," a.k.a. in-hospital patient transport. At that point, I had to buy pants, since they were required as part of my uniform.

That hospital became the first place I experienced all the social blunders so many of my peers had learned to navigate back in kindergarten. It had never occured to me to work through a disagreement with a person on my own. I would always run to tell our supervisor about the incident, as if I were tattling on my sister. I ended up with a lot of enemies, which meant the security guards got to know me pretty well during our evening walks to my mom's minivan. That job was where I met my first boyfriend. Come to think of it, it's also where I met my first husband. It's where I helped roll bodies (using a sheet so I wasn't actually touching them) in my first organ harvesting and saw my first autopsy. You know, the usual rights of passage for adolescents.

Though I slowly moved away from Homeschool Heather, it stuck with me for quite a while, becoming well-known enough that I was asked about the title in two completely different job interviews. Finally being able to refer to Homeschool Heather as someone who existed in the past-tense required a long road of making a lot of enemies, reading a ton of books written by actual Scientists, running thousands of ambulance calls, a couple of broken hearts, and a ton of therapy. At least I thought she was past-tense. Turns out changing my behaviors and putting on jeans wasn't enough. Homeschool Heather is also made up of thousands of thinking errors that slowly molded me.

Since I was the odd one out amongst all of my friends, for years I believed I knew what true oppression was. I don't. I know what religious oppression, gaslighting, and patriarchy feel like. Because I fought so hard to climb out of a social and educational pit, I thought everyone had the ability to do the same thing, if they would just acknowledge their oppression and stop making excuses. For some people, that's true. Hundreds of Exers have done it. Most of us have something else in common, though: we're White. My world was so small. I didn't climb out of my pit by myself. I had the advantage of a systemic rope to grab, with people at the top pulling me up to where society believed I should be. I only recently learned that not all of society believes everyone else should be there, too. Because I was blind to the world, I was blind to its evils.

That's not something from which I should have been sheltered, when awareness is what is needed. I wasn't sheltered from the devil; I was sheltered from the pure humanity of others. I had the advantage of breaking into a world in which feminists-the ones I feared in my diaries, had paved a smoother path for me to follow.

In the world of Homeschool Heather, oppression only took place between males and females, so I thought that was the only type there was. Now, I know that by believing that, I was ignoring others. In that ignorance, I was part of the racial and societal oppression that is actively destroying those around us.

While I've overcome Homeschool Heather, I don't want to abandon her completely. I don't get to leave her in the past by climbing out of the pit of oppression, walking away, and not looking back. Since I've climbed out, the myriad of other pits are visible and I'm realizing just how unfathomably deep they are. And no one climbs out alone. Now, as someone with privilege and agency, it's my job to hold the rope for others, while I toss dirt into every oppressive pit I can find. Grab a shovel.

6

Chasing Frisbees

"Have not I commanded thee? Be strong and of a good courage; be not afraid, neither be thou dismayed: for the Lord thy God is with thee whithersoever thou goest."

—Joshua 1:9, the verse I "claimed" as I embarked on
the pursuit of my biggest dream

I'd been to dozens of Children's Institutes throughout my childhood. It was the closest I'd ever get to being part of a class with an attendance greater than one. I lived for CIs. My AOL Instant Messenger screen name and first email address was "iluvCIs88." We never, ever took a family vacation that wasn't centered around a Basic or Advanced with a CI.

It was finally a place where I was without my parents for three hours a night, spending time with the Team Leaders, the coolest teenagers I'd ever met. I wanted to be just like them, with their perfectly tied neck bows, giant smiles, and Game Of Thrones extravagance-level hairstyles. I was the kid who spent the whole week practicing the songs and memorizing the verses that we would perform for the adults at the end of the week. But, more than any of that, I loved getting a good seat in large group (I think schools call them "assembly") when all the teams (classes) were together so I could watch the storyteller. The storyteller was one of the three to four people in their late teens/ early twenties who traveled the country running CIs when most people their age were in college.

I remember being at one of the smaller seminars where large-group took place in a cramped office filled with more kids than there were metal folding chairs. My team arrived for LG first. I'd tried to get my team a place near the front, but my leader was all about "the first being last" and made us sit in the back. I had to prevent Satan from building strongholds in my heart against her as I managed to stand on my tiptoes, high enough to see the storyteller tell my favorite CI story of all time.

Sure, ATI had hundreds of stories, but this was the first time I'd heard this one. I knew instantly I was destined to tell it. "The Frisbee Chasing Dog" had a repetitive catchphrase and audience participation, and as a human, I'm a big fan of instant gratification via positive feedback. This story wasn't groundbreakingly profound and had a fairly obvious plot; any storyline that began by learning to take instant, unquestioned instructions from authority would undoubtedly end with the protagonist suffering nearly devastating consequences if they failed to submit. Tale as old as cult.

I loved the way the storyteller delivered that story. I loved the way he was able to make me need to keep listening, even though I'd already guessed the ending—the frisbee-chasing dog had to choose between obeying his owner and chasing his frisbee. That is what I was meant to do.

I always paid close attention to ATI's stories, mostly so I could mimic the inflections and learn to deliver a compelling message. Every time my mother was in the shower, I would make my sister sit on the couch and listen to me practice, so I would be ready as soon as ATI asked me to travel with them. I'd practice leading the songs and teaching the hand motions opposite the audience (so they would use their right hand when I used my left).

Mostly, though, I practiced the stories. The more seminars I attended, the more stories I had for my audition plan. Every family was supposed to attend as many seminars as possible (if you skipped because you'd been to a Basic a dozen times already, that was Satan preventing your heart from hearing a message you'd never noticed before). This meant I eventually learned the varying styles of different people telling the same story.

Once a year, when all ATI members headed to Knoxville, sometimes the storyteller wasn't part of the traveling team, but an actual ATI founder himself. Hearing one of these stories told live by the author was my ultimate dream come true. Seeing him live did NOT disappoint. For me, it was unreal. Such passion in storytelling could only come from the mouth of the man who had lived through the true experience, having felt the conviction and pain only the protagonist could know.

When I was 12, my last year as a CI student, I sat in complete awe as my most admired Spiritual leader, the man who created Character First!, told us the story of his childhood habit. He chewed crayons and then showed his teacher a mouthful of masticated wax, while making what I can only imagine as the noise that inspired Jim Carrey's "Most annoying sound in the world."

He didn't simply tell the story. He chewed crayons during it. He peeled the paper like a banana as he spoke, pausing long enough to grab the room's attention, and then he'd snap off a bit with his teeth. He told us that while his teacher would spank him every time he chewed and showed his crayons, he'd never cared about the school spankings; he knew if he was spanked at school, the beatings waiting for him at home were going to be much worse.

As we, the audience, participated in the sounds and repetitive aspects, building our investment in his words, I took mental notes on his style. I grasped the edge of my carpet square as he described the dread he'd felt walking to his house to face his father.

His father asked him how school was and, at first, he omitted any wrongdoing, sticking merely to academics (the stories never focused too much on silly details like the importance of education, but kept them as small B-plots, necessary for story progression). Later that evening, the Crayon Chewer felt the weight only a Heavenly conviction can bring and went to confess his sin to his father. You see where this metaphor is going. As expected, his father brought him out behind the woodshed and slowly doffed his thick leather belt, curling it in his hands, as the young boy braced himself for what he knew would be the worst beating his father ever performed.

Our breath caught in our throats as he told us how he heard the belt "whoosh" in the air as it was raised above him and then... "CRACK!!" The belt finally made its stinging contact with skin, but our protagonist felt no pain. Again, he heard the "whoosh," followed by the anticipated "CRACK!" but felt nothing. He turned to look at his father and saw him weeping as he used the belt to beat his own leg, taking the punishment meant for his child. Subtle analogy, huh?

I'd heard that story several times in both the adult and children's seminars. It was on a solid rotation of altar-filling sermons, along with "The Wood Duck Story" (also by the Crayon Chewer), "The Pineapple Story" (my parents have this on VHS), "The Lost Pearl," and "Clanging Hangers."

These were the cult classics. I later learned this is an actual term for media geared towards a specific audience, but I mean it in the literal sense. This would have been convenient to know when I spent an embarrassing amount of time arguing with outsiders that films such as Monty Python and The Holy Grail or Clockwork Orange weren't even approved cult movies, let alone classics.

At the end of the Crayon story, I stood in line at the stage door for what felt like hours—ok, it was the staircase of a portable platform, but I'm trying to paint you a picture here—so I could spend a few minutes seeking the wisdom of my childhood hero (I typed "idol," but we all know I wasn't allowed to have those). When my turn finally came, he took out his pen and asked where I'd like him to sign my Bible.

I hated when fundie men expected the only thing I could want from them would be their signature. If people want their Bibles signed like yearbooks, that's their choice. I found it hypocritical to sign a book you were neither in, had written, nor were giving as a gift.

I asked him for recommendations on what I needed to do to become the Storyteller on The Children's Institute traveling team (CITT—it's going to come up a lot). He talked for a long time, repeating my name often, which I now recognize was a form of gaslighting, but at the time gave me a foreign feeling of actually being part of a conversation, not the receiving end of a sermon.

He told me the best way to discover if the CITT was part of God's plan for my life would be to spend time teaching CharacterFirst! under the leadership of the directors responsible for recruiting team members. I'd have to wait a few years, but that gave me time to hone my skills. They were going to love me.

* * *

When I was 17, I signed up to spend a semester in ATI's Oklahoma City training center. ATI put a lot of effort into talking us out of going to college and into working for them instead, because college "wastes the prime service years of a person's life." I didn't want to waste my life sitting in a pesky classroom doing humanistic quizzes like all those other kids. I was ready to max out my service years! It was well known that OKC was the most lenient of

ATI's training centers. I figured I'd be fine there, and it couldn't be as bad as the LIT center, since I was going voluntarily.

My father accompanied me on my first flight to deliver me to the training center safely, seeing as a woman should never travel without an authority. We landed amongst giant sculptures of arrows sticking out of the ground, which ATI insisted was not a symbol of the Indigenious people from whom we'd stolen the land, but a sign that ATI's ministry was needed in that city. How could we ignore the clear symbols calling the Quiverfullers to the area? We hopped into the standard ATI 15-passenger van in full Elder Price style, unaware that the next semester would open my eyes to ATI's despicable reality, turning my life-long dream into a nightmare.

The OKC training center had once been a hotel and still had its ghostly frame of extravagance. I could look around at the red-carpeted lobby with its gold fixtures and carved wood accents, envisioning the lavish events that once took place there. The ladies still wore long skirts, but ghosts of frills and lace had been replaced with oversized khaki hand-me-downs.

My father stayed that first night when everything seemed just as had been promised in ATI's monthly newsletter, Raising the Standard. He left the next day with a return ticket to accompany me back home in several weeks.

As with every ATI practice, once the parent had been successfully gaslit into believing this was the best thing for their child, the true oppression kicked in. It shocked me to find most of the parents had no idea how much abuse took place at the training centers. ATI promised parents a generation of young people who were pure and fully obedient to God, but the candy-coated brochures, and now websites, leave out the methods used to, in their words, "break a child's will."

A few years ago, a fellow Exer made a documentary, "The Cult Next Door", and I had my mother watch it with me. She was genuinely shocked by what she saw, while I nodded along, feeling exponentially validated. Even though she'd experienced ATI, she had no idea how truly evil they were. It was a completely different experience for a parent than it was for their child. Many of my friends entered ATI's training centers willingly, as I did, but either attempted suicide during their stay or came home with eyes now opened to the fact that we were completely trapped. Once in a while, we would hear stories of a student who attempted to escape from a training center. This should have been a red flag to everyone that these experiences were not equivalent to college, where walking a few blocks to Sonic is considered normal behavior and the faculty never uses the word "escape" when someone leaves campus.

I arrived after my roommate, which meant she had been able to claim the better part of the room with the window overlooking the parking lot. My bed was in the corner near the bathroom. Not only did Roommate get the better bed, she was a fervent Calvinist.

You would think that everyone would share the same religion in ATI, but they don't. ATI isn't a church; it's nondenominational, so people from many different sects are admitted, as long as they have the same basic fundamental belief that salvation is through Jesus, not good works, and they can afford the tuition.

I was a hardcore IFB at the time, as were most of the other people there. Basically, I believed God gave people free-will and we could change our own fate, and Roommate believed everything in the universe was predestined. As far as the Venn diagram of religions allowed in ATI went, Roommate and I were as far apart as you could get while still reading the same KJV Bible. (We found then deleted each other on social media a while ago and we're still polar opposites but for new reasons.) I'd shared rooms with River Bretheren who were a lot more flexible than she was (you probably gathered from context that was a pretty sick cult burn). It's fair to say we loathed each other. We were your typical "On Wednesdays, we debate predestination" 17-year-olds. We thought rooming with each other would be the worst part of our experience. We soon learned otherwise.

Our room was on the eighth floor, along with all the other girls. The boys occupied the third floor. No one was allowed to set foot on the floor assigned to the opposite gender except the maintenance guy, who had to be accompanied by two females. They intentionally put the girls on a much higher floor, so the boys would have no reason to pass by on their way up or downstairs. Once I showed up with my new-fangled ideas about equality, the boys were apparently no longer the only threat to avoiding all appearances of evil.

If I was going downstairs and the elevator stopped on the third floor, I behaved like a human, sharing the rest of the descent with the boy who also needed to go to the main floor. This behavior soon earned me a heart check. I was locked in my room with water and a Bible, with a staff member posted outside my door, so I could supposedly examine my heart for the root cause of my sinful elevator-riding etiquette. The boys never got heart checks for entering a girls' space (take that as innuendo-ish you will, it remains true); only the girls were punished for allowing ourselves to tempt the boys with our blouses' unpinned button gaps.

Even though they locked me in my room, I stand by the idea that this was the most lenient TC. Other Exers have told me how they'd been locked in cages in the basement of ATI headquarters for the exact same offense. As far as I know, there were no cages available in the once beautiful Oklahoma hotel.

The first two weeks were full-time training on how to teach CharacterFirst! I'd assumed it would be pretty self-explanatory; we'd be following and creating lesson plans, a skill in which all the eldest children were well-versed after having to homeschool ourselves and our younger siblings. But we had to learn how to gaslight. Since we couldn't bring up The Bible in public schools, we had to mask Biblical truths using animal stories. The goal was to get kids to ask about Bible stories because then it was legal to discuss God and attempt to convert them.

Most of that initial group was there just for the training and planned to use their training back in their hometowns. The people who were there just for the training were the "normal" ones, the ones who knew ATI was insane. They played by the rules at conferences but, at home, they wore jeans and watched movies, just complying enough to keep home tensions down until they could move out. These kids were known as the rebels, the ones Bill often warned us about. He would say that if there were two rebels in a large crowd, they would find each other, no matter what. He was right; I found the other one.

It was easy to spot him. He got in trouble on day one for wearing zip-off pants; apparently, they gave off "skater" vibes—I don't know—but the leaders were having no part of it. The Rebel and I quickly realized that things here were much worse than we'd imagined. We'd gone in expecting to be slightly inconvenienced by ATI's strict rules but found ourselves trapped in a world where the goal was to break us. I remember being annoyed at how extremely attracted I was to The Rebel (we spoke in song lyrics that no one else should have known... how could I not have wanted to get into those zip-off cargo pants?) and we agreed that, in a normal world, we would have gone on a date.

Since many of us had been kept hidden for most of our lives, etiquette classes were required so we could learn society's norms for human interaction. We learned how to set a table and the order in which to use our forks. The Rebel and I did a decent job of playing it cool until it was time to learn proper male/female table etiquette.

We volunteered to be the examples, mostly because everyone else was shy and we wanted to get to Wednesday night hymn-sing on time. Also, we knew it was the closest we'd get to going on a date.

ATI taught us it was customary for a handshake only to be initiated by the female, so everyone gasped as I extended my hand to him. That put me on the radar for being a "Jezebel" because now everyone knew I was not amongst the girls who had vowed never to touch a man before marriage. Oops.

I was instructed not to appear too flirtatious when The Rebel pulled out my chair and I smoothed my skirt down over my sinful tush—you know, the way everyone does when they're about to sit in a skirt. We made eye contact throughout our mimed meal and ended the interaction with a bow and curtsy, the most casual way to bid a date adieu.

I thought class had gone well but was pulled aside to be admonished for having been far too comfortable in a situation dining with a man. I was in trouble for doing the thing I was supposed to be learning. The Rebel aced that test, as well, but only I was pulled aside, seeing as his ease clearly stemmed from my inviting attitude. The Rebel is the only guy from ATI who has ever recognized the patriarchy and directly apologized to me for it before getting out.

When those first two weeks ended and the training group packed up, reality set in for me that I'd be trapped there all alone. On the day they left, in what was probably my most rebellious moment on ATI turf, The Rebel and I rendezvoused in the stairway on the second floor landing. We had to pick a secluded location where we were both allowed, that had enough plausible deniability for us to claim we simply passed each other on the stairs. It had to be the second floor because he had no reason to go higher than the third, and stopping on the first or third floors would give us no warning if someone was entering the stairway.

The second floor was rarely used and the only one we would both feasibly pass.

We made sure no one else was using the stairs, and then, we finally did it. We hugged! It was the one thing I did on purpose that could have ruined my entire chance at making the traveling team. Now that you've all been through quarantine, I feel like you'll understand my deep, burning need for a few seconds of holding a person you were forbidden from touching. We decided to go all in, skipping the courtship side-hug and went right for the full-embrace hug, reserved especially for marriage. I guess they were right about that handshake being a slippery slope.

We were about to share our first kiss ever for both of us, when someone started coming down from the third floor. We quickly made our way apart in opposite directions, knowing that once he was gone, I'd have no one left there who made me feel safe.

* * *

I was left with the CF! Team and three full-time training center staff members who admittedly hated it there but found it better than homeschooling their younger siblings. Most of the CF! Team (and most ATI students) come from lower income families who can't pay the full price of TC "tuition," so we signed up for a discount on our room and board in exchange for cooking and cleaning. It was only a few hundred off the tuition, so I assumed the work would be a few hours a week. This ended up being ATI's way of paying only three full-time staff members while the students worked for less than minimum wage, which ATI excuses as "character-building exercises," intentionally stripping their followers of any free will.

I should have seen this coming. Scattered throughout ATI's seminars and teachings, you'll find the repetition of brainwashing us out of our autonomy. Wisdom Booklet 18's homework assignment included listing "rights." ATI places the quotation marks because they are professional gaslighters.

They provided a small list of examples of "rights" we needed to yield in order to get our creative juices flowing. Some of their examples—with zero hyperbole from me—include our rights to listen to any music we like, choose our own clothes, eat good meals we enjoy, spend our own money, be helped with chores, be treated with proper manners, be free from injury, make our own decisions, choose our own friends, be heard without interruption (#MrVicePresidentImSpeaking), be appreciated, not be nagged, have our own space, and relax. Now, of course, sometimes we don't have these things, but that doesn't mean we, or anyone, is undeserving of them, any of them. Each training center leader's goals were to ensure that each of us had yielded our rights and to do everything in their power to break us.

There were no set hours for chores. The rule was that any of us could be expected to stop whatever we were doing to cheer-fully complete the request of a leader, unless we were actively eating in the dining hall. Chores were assigned based on what The Lord told the leaders we needed to be doing and, of course, our gender. Boys were assigned the masculine work: landscaping, vehicle, and building repairs. I was assigned to the feminine tasks of scrubbing bathrooms, washing and folding all of the TC's linen, or hand polishing the wood paneling.

My favorite assignment was vacuuming, because it meant I couldn't hear anyone tell me that bending over to move the plug caused yet another boy to stumble Spiritually. I pretended to enjoy doing the dishes because that was—and always has been— my least favorite chore of all time. I didn't need God telling anyone to make me do dishes more often.

I didn't mind the chores themselves so much and was more than willing to work for a fair trade of the tuition discount, but I had never intended to be their Cinderella. They sold this experience to families as an alternative to college; I was there to learn to teach in a classroom, not to polish baseboards. They really liked the idea of military discipline and instant, unquestioned, frisbee-chasing obedience, and would demonstrate that by pulling us away from lesson planning or out of bed early to do chores.

It didn't take long for me to hate every second I existed there. No wonder so many others attempted suicide on their watch. I needed any hint of solace and found the only way I could to become off-limits to their power; I ate. They had full control of when I slept, showered, called home, dressed, read, my teaching style, what (and obviously who) I put in my vagina, and who I had as friends. The only thing I could control anymore was my food - or so I thought.

There were six seating times for meals each day, two for each meal. I was allowed to be there for all seating times, as long as I didn't sit at a table alone with a boy and didn't join a table of already-seated boys without another girl to accompany me. Often, I'd end up sitting at a table alone, but at least that meant I was in control of something. Food became my only escape. I gained 50 pounds in the three months I was there.

Every two weeks, our team was allowed a group trip to Walmart. We requested a Target run, but they openly stand by the LGBTQ+ community, their logo is a circle- allegedly the Devil's favorite shape, and say "Happy Holidays" (which might as well be a Satanic ritual in cult standards), so, off we went, to the store that sabotages their employees' healthcare plans and has aisles of firearms.

Planning transportation was the most time-consuming aspect of these endeavors because we couldn't just get into the giant van and find a seat. It was an algorithm each time, depending on who needed to go on the adventure. If both males and females were going, there needed to be at least two of each. If the van was at capacity and a male and female had to sit together, they either needed to be married, parent and child, or siblings—not that being any of those combinations kept them from raping each other.

No one assigned seats, which would have been the most logical option, so we had to do seat math every time we left the building. Our team had 13 girls and 3 boys. 2 of the boys had at least 1 sister on the team. There was only 1 sibling-less boy who needed to sit on an end. It should not have been this difficult.

Once we arrived at Walmart, we were allowed to separate into same-sex groups. I always stuck with Rachel because she wore eyeliner and was my best chance at a friend who hadn't finished yielding all of her rights to autonomy yet (I was right, she's a badass). It never took long to grab essentials, so we spent most of our time looking at clothes, which eventually became essential for me after I outgrew everything I'd packed. On our October trip, Rachel and I made the bold move of buying matching black skirts with asymmetrical hemlines. They looked like witch skirts and it was the closest we could get to acknowledging Halloween in a way that didn't require us to tell children that their innocent acts of masked gluttony were a ticket straight to Hell.

During one of our shopping trips, I loaded up on non-perishable, emotional-void-filling snacks I could keep under my bed, and a box of tampons. The leaders sorted through our bags once we finished shopping, in order to assure we did not bring anything sinful back to the training center. That's when they discovered my tampons, which I hadn't tried to hide since it seemed like a standard item to have.

The box was immediately confiscated, and I was locked in my room for another heart check, where I was ordered to repent from any enjoyment I may have experienced during previous tampon insertion and removal (I'm not sure what they'd heard about tampons but, judging by their lecture, it was fairly apparent they had never used one) and for robbing my future husband of his right to break my hymen. I asked why my future husband didn't have to yield his right to my hymen when I was supposed to be yielding all of my rights, which only got my door locked for longer.

While I was admonished for my careless, selfish behavior of taking my own virginity (I know that's not how it works but they weren't having it), so many of the other girls at the training center were never able to make that choice themselves, after their older brothers sexually assaulted them.

That sentence is a lot, right? You would think it would at least be followed by a full stop. But they would say it as if sibling rape was just an unfortunate part of childhood, like skinned knees or having to finish your dinner before having dessert. As it turned out, sibling rape was far more common in ATI than I had ever imagined. We ended up talking about it in a few of our Wisdom Searches, and going around the room discussing what each girl did that caused her brother to sin, using ATI's chart on counseling sexual assault as a guide.

Now, if any of you know me, you know I have the worst poker face and react rather expressively to things. Picture yourself watching that scene in A Handmaid's Tale where the exact same thing takes place, but you're living it. This is why I can't watch that show. It's too real. I've lived those scenes.

I sat next to those girls as they confessed what they thought may have led to their attacks, like that time they wore a nightgown that was perhaps too thin, allowing their brother to see their body underneath, or a favorite shirt that was now too tight for their growing breasts. One had forgotten to bring her clean clothes into the bathroom with her and had to walk back to her room in a towel after her shower. She admitted this was likely too much temptation for her pubescent brothers, who started molesting her not long after. Unable to contain my silence any longer, I said that none of those things justified their brothers' actions. None of this was their fault.

My worldly suggestions were quickly dismissed, due to my lack of understanding since the obvious reason I had been spared was I didn't have a brother. I was again shown ATI's algorithm for counseling sexual abuse, which directs the victim to find how they brought it upon themselves and how to be grateful to their attacker for giving them the ability to become mighty in spirit. I earned myself another heart check for trying to usurp ATI's teachings during Wisdom Search.

* * *

Finally, the time came for us to go into actual schools and teach classes on character. We knew we weren't allowed to talk about anything involving the Bible, which everyone proudly accepted as their own personal martyr assignment. I had never been into a school full of kids before. I'd been inside a school to see high school plays or go with my parents to vote, and tried to savor every embodiment of the surroundings in those few minutes. I'd recognize the lockers from my mother's black-and-white yearbook photos, surprised to find they were bright orange in real life. I'd go to the bathroom more often than I needed, so I could pretend to borrow someone's lipstick to impress the football team and gossip about who got pinned. Yeah, it sounds ridiculous because it is. I still have no concept of what it's like to attend school, so I pulled what fantasies I could from The Breakfast Club and Bye, Bye, Birdie.

This was the first time I had been amongst real teachers and classes. I watched, feeling the weight of overwhelming betrayal that comes with discovering everything you were told had been a lie. School wasn't evil.* Teachers loved their students and actually cared about them. Those kids had parents who loved them. School wasn't the punishment I had always believed. Nothing I could tell these kids would be relatable, and I was too busy asking first graders to tell me about the magic of being picked for the school play to remember I was there to teach them about loyalty, based on how nice geese are to each other.

I had no idea what to do in this world until... it happened, the one thing I did best. It was time to belt out a Broadway musical number! I'm told this is not done in schools nation-wide but, in Oklahoma, they start the school day by saying the Pledge of Allegiance, singing the National Anthem, and then singing their official State song. The song is none other than "Oklahoma," which I'd learned from years of folding laundry next to my grandma's 8-track player. The school had choreographed moves and everything! After having been my only experience in a true school setting, I refuse to believe that plays like Hairspray, Grease, and The Prom are anything less than documentaries. If ATI wanted to prevent me from romanticizing public schools, they shouldn't have dropped me into a live musical. Of course, my joy was short-lived. I went straight into a heart check for knowing the words to a song from a worldy play that encouraged dating and humorized promiscuity.

Every day, after 90 glorious seconds of unison participation in the sinful culture that is Broadway music, we would go from class to class teaching Bible stories disguised as tales of character-building animals. Sometimes, we would catch the end of a regular class. It was astonishing to me that kids so young were learning so much. Third graders knew things I hadn't learned until I was a teenager. Kindergarteners knew how to identify and process their emotions without waiting for a rhema. Second graders informed me that Europe is not a country. I'm sure my mother taught me about continents versus countries, but that stuff gets blurred when the invention of the euro sends the church into a tailspin and you're immersed in sermons about living in fulfilled prophecies and told nothing matters because you're about to get raptured anyway.

Those kids amazed me and I became infinitely angry over having been robbed of an education. I was terrified to tell these kids anything, because I didn't want anyone to find out I wasn't smart, especially the kids who expected me to teach them. That fear still remains, as I'll often find myself fascinated by my kids' online classes and constantly discover how much I didn't know that I didn't know.

About halfway through the semester, I was assigned the humility versus pride lesson. I was paired that week with the Douche of Patriarchy. Once we got our team assignments, I walked over to him and asked when he wanted to go over the lesson plan. He told me not to worry about it; since we were a co-ed team, he would do all the teaching and I'd just have to support everything he said. I wasn't having that and he eventually agreed to let me teach one class, just to shut me up. Then, he ran to his sister, a leader, to tattle on me about how forward I was with my petulant questions on the lesson plans. His sister sat outside my door for that heart check and forbade me from vacuuming or polishing the wainscoting on the third floor—just in case I was planning on tempting more of the guys by existing.

The Douche of Patriarchy taught most of the classes that week, and I taught one. We hadn't seen each other's plans. I spent part of mine focusing on why humility is not the same as low self-esteem or hiding your talent, and why it's wrong to be prideful but good to take pride in your work. The leaders confirmed this is why women shouldn't usurp men, as I should have been teaching that all pride is sinful, and I was reassigned to the more feminine role of crafts.

I've blocked out so much of my experience in OKC. I know I had to smile when I didn't mean it. I remember having to find ways to enhance my countenance with my hair tied back after I ended up with a raging lice infestation. I remember one girl made a "16 going on 17" dress for another girl's birthday, and I loved watching her do cartwheels in the eighth floor hallway, since that was the only place she was allowed to wear such a promiscuous garment. I remember going to a farm one weekend and attempting to go across the zipline, but I fell right into the rocky water halfway across and lost the phone that my father had appealed to let me have. The mother of the head TC family drove me back to the TC to get dry clothes, using the entire drive to lecture me on what sin in my life had caused me to fall.

What lesson was God trying to teach me? Was this a result of my rebellious attitude? Turns out the incident was on video and the Douche of Patriarchy can be seen laughing and aggressively shaking the rope as I rode across. Our fathers spent a lot of time yelling over the phone about this (he totally should have paid for that phone replacement AND said he was sorry), but it ended with it being my fault for having pestered him about lesson plans.

I remember having to borrow a larger-than-I-had-packed red shirt for our team photo requiring fall-themed colors. For that photo, they had us walk down to the site of the OKC bombing and do a photo shoot by the reflecting pool. I remember cringing at how incredibly disrespectful that was. I remember sitting on the TC's landing between the first and second floors, at the long desk divided into three sections, a phone in each one that could only make collect calls. I'd always sit on an end; in case a guy needed to use a phone, we could have a seat between us and I wouldn't get locked in my room again. I was social-distancing way before it was a safety issue. I'd cry while I listened to my sister play "Home For The Holidays" on the piano because I'd be home for Thanksgiving.

I remember all I wanted was for this terrible experience to have been worth it, to finally land a spot on the CITT. I know there are memories I'm omitting, but so many of those cards from my brain's rolodex are stuck together. I know they're there, but I can't see them.

Finally, the last day of teaching came. I was already packed to leave the next day and mentally checked out, but then the storyteller had an emergency. We were scheduled to manage the school assembly and none of the guys knew the story. I ended up taking to the stage as the storyteller. The entire reason I'd gone out there and stayed for the duration was to earn my spot on the traveling team. This was my moment and you can bless your assurance that I was ready. I'd been admonished for practicing stories more often than I'd spent mandatorily memorizing Psalm 37 and now was the time to prove it had been worth it all; as we had sung for Bill every time he demanded an encore of his favorite hymn: "When We See Christ".

I got up in front of those hundreds of kids and I told the most engaging tale of "The Frisbee Chasing Dog" a woman has ever told. And I loved it. Time stood still as everything I had wanted was finally happening and I was crushing it without an ounce of humility. I was good and I knew it.

I bet that right before the first time I'd heard that story, the storyteller prayed, asking God to use him as the vessel to speak to a child's spirit. I believe God fulfilled his prayer, although I was not obliged to blind obedience as he was intending. No, no. In fact, it was the beginning of my journey to overcome the person the cult was trying to create, although I'd had to go all the way in before realizing I needed to get out. It taught me that if I could pour all of myself into my story, it was possible to ignite an emotional connection with a stranger in a way nothing else can. I was going to be the one who could inspire a captivated audience, damnit.

At the end of the semester, one by one, we sat with the directors for evaluation, to see if they agreed on the path we felt

God was calling us—basically, the American Idol of cults. I sat across from their desk and, even though they couldn't see my legs, I made sure to sit like a modest lady with crossed ankles, not knees. I remembered to smile because lice don't enhance your countenance. I handed them my self-evaluation, filled with the most spiritually guided answers I've probably ever written. They had to see how bold, flexible, loyal, creative, enthusiastic, and genuine I was! I had to be all they'd ever wanted.

I knew I was born to tell stories, to inspire people to get up and do something they never thought possible.

And then they crushed me.

I was a girl. Not ONCE in more than half of my life spent dreaming that dream did it occur to me that the storyteller was always a man. It truly never crossed my mind that I had never seen a woman tell a story. The woman always taught and led the songs. The only gender-neutral team member was the piano player. I didn't play the piano. I didn't want to teach songs, nor did anyone want to hear me sing. They had seen me jump in and flawlessly take over that assembly at a moment's notice. They knew how hard I had worked to get there. But none of that mattered.

The storyteller was a representation of a pastor, a spiritual leader, and women were not capable of filling that role.

On the flight home, I sat straight up, so as not to spread my lice to the next person to fill my seat, staring out over the clouds, over the rainbows, whisper-singing my "mission" song, as I wept over my shattered dream.

From that moment, I knew I needed a bigger dream, one that didn't require the permission of someone else.

*I acknowledge the deep, unforgivable trauma that abounds in a school setting. My small observation is not intended to invalidate anyone's experience.

Me, age 11, with Bill Gothard

Annual ATI family photo, 1999. We made sure to wear
the ATI pins in most of our photos.

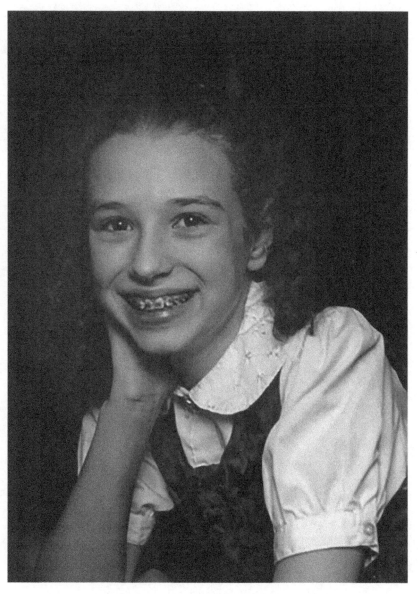

My photo alone, to show I wasn't a rebellious ATI student

Knoxville, 2002

My only time on a school bus; on the shuttle for COMMIT.
Knoxville, circa 2003

My annual ATI photo, age 14

My sister as a student, and me,
as a Team Assistant at a Children's Institute, circa 2005

My mother, almost at the front of the line to meet Bill, circa 1998

Our yearly ATI family photo, 2004

My annual ATI photo, age 16. Note the humble brag background:
The photo of me with Bill, a print of his Psalm 1 chalk talk,
and our ATI certificate.

7

Craving Trauma

*"The pectoral muscles are paralyzed and the intercostal muscles are
unable to act. Air can be drawn into the lungs, but cannot be exhaled.
Finally, carbon dioxide builds up in the lungs and in the bloodstream
and the cramps partially subside... Then another agony begins. A deep
crushing pain deep in the chest as the pericardium slowly fills with serum
and begins to compress the heart. The compressed heart is struggling to
pump heavy, thick, sluggish blood into the tissues—the tortured lungs
are making a frantic effort to gasp in small gulps of air."*

—The Crucifixion of Jesus, Men's Manual Vol. 1

People love to ask, "What made you want to become a medic?"
They always expect some heroic answer about wanting to
give back to the community, or some assumed story about my
brush with death that I only survived after vowing to spend my
life saving others. They never really know how to react when
the answer they hear is, "I needed to escape from a cult but I'm
uncomfortable in safe environments and REALLY good at making fast friends with strangers."

EMS is what saved me, not by transporting me to a hospital,
but by transporting me into a world where women - where I - could
lead and be seen as equal. I'd never be able to be the storyteller

on the traveling team but, with each 911 call, I could travel into someone's story and change their narrative.

Actually, ATI had more to do with inspiring my EMS career than they had intended. My desire to learn how to run towards a crisis when everyone else was running away was ignited during my very first ATI conference, as I sat listening to Mickey Bonner preach. I don't remember much of his sermon other than feeling like he was screaming at me, and I didn't like it. Then, he said, "We must learn to pray with the mind of Christ and it comes only when we humble ourselves before Him. It comes only when we are broken." And then, he dropped dead.

The ALERT guys jumped onto the stage and began CPR in front of 1,400 people, who coped by singing "Amazing Grace."

(Pro tip: Singing while doing CPR is extremely handy for keeping up a 100-beats-per-minute rhythm, but I'd stick to "Stayin' Alive" or "Dancing Queen." The slow beat of "Amazing Grace" promotes fatigue. Eventually, someone figured out that you can sing "Amazing Grace" to the tune of the Gilligan's Island theme song, which meant that you could have a fast enough CPR beat while avoiding rock music's path to Hell, especially when face-to-face with death's grasp.)

We were all told to pray. Fourteen hundred of us all prayed as we watched the ALERT guys taking turns pressing their inter-laced fingers against the preacher's sternum. It was then that I decided praying is only a solution when you are truly unable to be a part of the answer. I don't get my kids a drink or a snack when they are capable of doing it themselves, and I have much less going on than God does. Why would God magically solve a problem for you when you should be the one doing something about it? I can't bring myself to sit and pray when I can be part of the answer. I would have been perfectly happy to join ALERT but, alas, since ATI forbade that, the secular route of EMS was my only other option.

I've always felt incredibly at home in a hospital environment, especially when it's chaotic. I love the emergency room. Ever since I can remember, I've spent hours sitting by my paternal grandma in the ER when she would "have a spell," which is what she called fainting. We would go through the usual routine of calling family members with updates and figuring out which of us was going to stay with Grandma for the next few days to make sure she was alright. Most often, that task fell to my mom, which meant I also stayed there.

The older I got, the more I was able to help. When I was 16, Grandma's spells went from something that would happen if she was upset and not eating or drinking to much more frequent, unpredictable incidents, making it unsafe for her to live alone. My sister was 9, and it would have been a lot of added stress on Grandma to have my mom there while trying to homeschool two kids. My cousins had young kids, so I was the one who ended up moving in with Grandma to care for her full time. I'd spent enough time listening to the ER staff go over everything with my family that I was well-versed in the language and warning signs for emergencies. Not to mention, since no one felt like giving me "the talk," outside of being terrified after hearing in the Basic seminar that oral gives you throat cancer, I'd pulled our giant medical encyclopedias off the shelf and taught myself enough to know the actual science behind making a human. The encyclopedias were riveting, and I'm pretty sure I read them cover to cover.

Moving in with her, I knew there was a very good chance I would be the one to discover Grandma when she transformed from a person to a body, and I had made peace with that. My maternal grandfather had died when I was 9 and I remember sitting alone in his room with him while we waited for the coroner. Looking back, it's kind of weird that everyone let a kid hang out in the room with a dead guy. But, hey, on the scale of things my parents thought were beneficial to me, that one wasn't that bad; it ended up actually beneficial for my career. I've been attending open casket funerals and wakes since I was a toddler. It's never easy to see someone who was a person with a life full of everything we experience become a body when the next breath didn't come; but being comfortable discovering a body (or parts) after they have died an extremely unfortunate death, sometimes weeks before we get there, has a bit less of a sting after being exposed to death scattered throughout my childhood.

When I moved in with Grandma, it became almost impossible for my mom to keep up with homeschooling me. I was getting frustrated by falling behind in what I knew was an already-stunted education. I ended up taking the teacher's videos and Parent Guide Planners, so I could homeschool myself in the down time when Grandma didn't need help. I quickly learned that if I used the closed caption, I could sneak into the TV room after Grandma was in bed, watch ahead in the videos, and read in the waiting room of her doctor's appointments and hospital stays, so I could "graduate" a year early.

My only down time was when I was volunteering as a candy striper at the hospital where I'd also be able to duck out to spend time in Grandma's room. I was still the super weird girl who wore a flowing, ankle-length skirt, rather than khaki pants like everyone else. But, even so, the people I met as a candy striper may have been the most influential ones in the process of overcoming Homeschool Heather.

I soon became close friends with Brandon, who led our volunteer orientation and was already involved in EMS. He was the first guy who ever hit on me not using chickens or secret plans to sit near each other during hymn-sing to do so. He knew I really wanted to get into EMS so, instead of plagiarizing a bunch of songs, he brought me his biology book, simultaneously teaching me how to handle emergencies and giving me "the talk" (which I was shocked to find didn't include the "fact" about women being allergic to semen before they are married).

Holding a high school textbook was the type of excitement I imagine girls felt when they saw The Beatles from the front row. All of this youthful excitement was a lot to suppress while having to be the girl who was very successfully parentified. I became instantly obsessed with learning what makes bodies work the way they do and the fascinating mechanisms behind physical symptoms. Knowing why Grandma needed electrolytes to exist when she didn't even play football absolutely blew my mind. If I took out the patriarchal gaslighting attempts instructing husbands and fathers to control all medical decisions from each Wisdom Booklet's "Medicine Resource," I could pull enough physiological facts to allow myself to become mesmerized by the few table scraps of science they tossed my way. ATI's first aid course was fully centered around The Good Samaritan; I find it ironic that the law protecting lay people who attempt to help in an emergency is called "The Good Samaritan Law." Learning that made it much more difficult to separate Biblical lessons from the ones the American Heart Association teaches.

Thanks to Wisdom Booklet 29's fairly accurate instructions on brain function after injury and what I'd picked up from my secret candy-striping biology lessons between filling water pitchers and tucking perfect hospital corners, I knew exactly what to do that day I was following Grandma down the hall to the TV room for her afternoon programs. She collapsed to one side, I dropped her tray of lunch, and she had her first stroke in my arms.

By the time the ambulance arrived, her symptoms had subsided and she insisted she was fine. Grandma was an extremely proper lady who would insist her pantyhose be put on before the ambulance arrived, knowing they would just be cut for the EKG monitor leads to stick to her ankles. It didn't matter; what mattered was that she had been classy at the time of her crisis. I knew her sudden onset and resolution of symptoms was consistent with a Transient Ischemic Attack (TIA), and she knew I wasn't about to let her use her now-clear speech to talk her way out of going to a hospital.

The ER doctor came by her room after a few hours to tell me she had, in fact, suffered a stroke, and had it not been for my insistence and knowledge of what was happening, it may have gone undiagnosed. That stroke was the beginning of the end. Stroke after stroke, I rode with her in the ambulance and, each time, I was fascinated by the way the crew moved with such flow, as if they were performing a well-choreographed dance routine. Their calm, swift actions drew me in as I would watch them write down all her information on their gloves. It's a tiny action that drew me to the wonder of EMS from the beginning. That was the coolest thing I had ever seen, and now I do it on every single call.

A few more frequent strokes and heart attacks left Grandma with severe physical deficits. She had to have a feeding tube placed. This was heartbreaking; she had spent a lifetime with the talent of timing each and every dish perfectly to come out at the right temperature, all at once, in order to create the perfect Sunday dinner each and every week, no matter what she cooked.

I went to sleep that night knowing that the next day, I'd be heading to see her in room 186, bed 2, to learn how to manage her tube so she could return home. But I woke to the phone ringing at 3:30 a.m., to tell us Grandma had gone into cardiac arrest and been pronounced dead the next moment, after they mixed up her chart with the one of her roommate, which had "DNR" on its cover. Since I was unfortunately relieved of the full-time responsibility of caring for Grandma, I was free to explore the mesmerizing world of EMS. Grandma left me her double-stranded pearl necklace and $450 to take the EMT class at the station down the street, after being the only one to witness my glimpse into a world in which I could thrive.

I signed up for the Explorer Post and the next EMT class they were having. On my very first night at Explorer Post, I learned how to intubate (place a breathing tube in someone's airway) and, later, got in trouble for leaving the handout of the instructions on the dining room table; when you're the head officer of purity culture, it's easy to confuse a diagram of vocal cords with that of a vagina.

I didn't just learn one of the most difficult skills I'd ever use, I also met Danielle. She was my age, but had much more of her shit together. She was already an EMT with plans to become a doctor and taught a lot of the practical (hands-on) stations for the classes. She, like most people who met me, realized quickly that I was pretty sheltered and had no idea what being a teenager was like. She never tried to change me, but she did take me shopping to prove I wouldn't instantly burst into flames if I owned a pair of jeans. She showed me it was not only possible, but very normal, for a woman to have or even take over control of everyone on a scene. A few months later, I passed my EMT exam and "graduated" ATI a year ahead of schedule after doubling up on homeschooling myself.

I started riding the ambulance every Monday night with Danielle, and (gasp!) two guys our age. Not long after turning 18, I also joined the ambulance service where Brandon worked. I was finally a part of that wonder that comes with walking into someone else's world and transitioning into that choreographed dance around death without saying a word.

When "The Unbreakable Kimmy Schmidt" premiered, I was often asked if it was based on me. Honestly, it could have been. All those interactions she has where she thinks she's playing it totally cool, but everyone around her has no idea what she's talking about... Welcome to my life.

I rolled up on one of my first calls ever for "the unresponsive party on the sidewalk." I was all amped up, ready to jump in with the defibrillator and be the hero, but it turns out the man was just taking a nap. As we loaded the very sleepy man into the ambulance, the cops joked, "Well, we found the little bit he had left in his car. Looks like he had way too much wild turkey again," and my mind flooded with excitement over knowing exactly what the problem was! This was one of the science facts I knew! But even though I knew how tired I got after a Thanksgiving dinner loaded with tryptophan, I couldn't imagine how anyone could eat enough wild turkey to alter their mental status. After I gave my first extremely confident patient diagnosis to the doc at the ER, I learned what whiskey was.

For those first few years, I felt like I was living two completely separate lives. There was the church's Homeschool Heather, who tried her best to be what they wanted but constantly fell short, and the World's Homeschool Heather, who no one thought would make it. I knew I belonged in that World; I'd just figured it out faster than they did. Every Sunday, I would ride on the church's red bus through the neighborhoods stereotyped with violence and poverty (you know, prime mission field) to pick up "The Bus Kids" for church. It wasn't unusual for the bus to have to pull over, so the city's ambulance could blaze past us with our same mission of loading up our vehicle, in hopes someone will be saved. I'd look out the windows to see the ambulance speeding past, feeling like one of those scenes in a movie, where everything around me freezes as I'm compelled to burst out in song about how there's so much more out there for me. I'd have to shake myself back to reality, knowing that, somehow, I'd have to break out of this world and into the one where I knew I belonged.

The most difficult aspect wasn't so much learning how to be an EMT or even dealing with the gore. The blood never bothered me, anyway. It was constantly coming face-to-face with a conviction I didn't know the church had convinced me to believe until, in that split second, I would have to decide if I believed my actions would condemn me to Hell and if I was willing to risk it to save the life right in front of me.

People will ask why I got into EMS if I knew it would go against my beliefs. Those people have obviously never been through the process of deconstructing cult trauma. (I typed that after I decided it wouldn't be good for publicity to call them idiots. Those questions always make me incredibly angry, even when they are asked with the purest of intentions, but angry or not, I don't believe name-calling is ever a productive behavior). I knew I'd have to go against the cult's standards, like wearing pants and riding alone in a car with a boy, but, medically, I thought everything would be fine because both sides were pro-life, right? Selah.

I know only the very religious amongst you will understand what I mean by that, but that's ok; that's why it's there. The ones who don't get it are probably actually pro-life.

When I filled out the applications to join each ambulance company, they asked things like, "Is there anything that would prevent you from performing the tasks expected of you?" Normally, I'd write that I have well-controlled asthma, I'm a weak swimmer, and, sometimes, I faint like a goat if I get stressed or my period is too heavy. (Before I got birth control, I just couldn't drive on days I had my period, which was a fun way to sign up for shifts and get over any stigma that periods should be something my guy friends shouldn't hear about.) It never dawned on me to write, "I have some deeply rooted religious trauma, probably traced back to Levitical law, which will make me draw some fine mental lines surrounding time of death, in order to comply with the cult's doctrine."

And that's how I found myself standing in the doorway of an apartment, sniffing the putrid stench of rotting flesh, holding the skin of a degloved arm on the end of my EKG wire. I'd gotten around it before. If nothing else, cult kids are great at loopholes. I knew I would be marked unclean for eternity in the eyes of God if I touched a dead body so, at my first job where I did hospital patient transport and sometimes had to take bodies to the morgue, I figured I'd be ok if I just touched the body bag and the metal cart, never the actual body. That's why I panicked hard when My Teenage Crush and I were bringing a body to the morgue and the arm ripped the body bag open. My Teenage Crush tucked the arm back, but I was terrified he was now in for some hardcore repenting after saving me the burden of touching a dead body. It's really easy to be seen as a Disney Prince when you're around a girl who can see her whole life in Mother Gothel's lies.

Sometimes, at that job, they would ask us if anyone wanted to help with the organ harvestings (Brandon and I always said yes, and I know it's confusing but we worked at several jobs together) and we would have to help turn the bodies and position them for the surgeons in the morgue. I always made sure I was lifting with a sheet or a towel, so I was never in contact with the dead body. I had tried to justify to myself that gloves would take care of that Levitical law. But then again, I figured if that was true, sex with a condom wouldn't actually count as sex, and the world seemed to think that counted, so I guess my glove loophole was out.

I decided it would be fine to perform CPR because, if I was doing CPR, they weren't technically dead "yet," so it was still Levitically legal. If it was just body parts, that was fine, because they might be used for organ harvesting. If I had to pronounce them dead, it was still ok for me to put the EKG monitor on them, to confirm a flat line; they wouldn't be permanently defined as dead until I said it, so it was ok to touch them for the evaluation. Making up all these arbitrary rules came quite naturally to me after hearing countless sermons on why Christians

should boycott Starbucks, while the preacher's white cup bran-
dishing the green "demonic siren" sat on the pulpit.

What people don't realize—and I didn't realize until my
therapist, Paula, let me borrow her copy of "The Body Keeps
The Score" by Dr. Bessel van der Kolk—is that although going
from a cult to EMS may seem counterintuitive to many, it really
was a natural progression. Dr. van der Kolk writes about a study
done on mice who were raised in a nurturing environment and
some who were raised in a chaotic environment, both placed in
a stressful situation and given the option of retreat to either of
the environments. Each group returned to the environment most
similar to the one in which they were raised, even though one
option was clearly more nurturing.

The mice, much like humans, will return to what's familiar,
rather than venturing into the unknown. When Paula showed
me that, I felt like it all made sense. I'll never be able to find
peace in the world of white picket fences and perfectly mani-
cured lawns, but stick me in a smashed-up car, hidden under a
blanket with a hysteric, trapped driver, as we listen to the jaws
of life spray broken shards of windshield over us, and I find my
calm. The Bible is jam-packed with gore and illness and they
told me to find comfort within its pages, so, really, this is their
fault for not being more specific.

The Wisdom Booklets' "Medicine Resource" is probably the
most factual subject they taught; the catch was they had to pull
every lesson from the Bible. I remember feeling immense guilt over
it, but not being able to stop reading the deep dive they did into
the pathophysiology of crucifixion. Jesus' death on the cross was
just a fact of Christianity, not something we ever explored on a
physical level of the internal process the body experiences during its
slow journey towards death. I knew at His moment of death, "He
gave up the ghost," which made its way into my mind as finally
letting himself die, like when people hold onto life a little longer

just to see someone once more. I thought His final cause of death was the spear stabbed through His side and the cross was just what they did then for torture until the person starved to death.

But it's so much more metabolically complex than that! The Wisdom Booklet's lesson is quite graphic, beginning with the intentional way a person was nailed to a cross, the arms not spread in a full span to allow for flexion. With the fatigue of the arms, comes intense muscle cramps, resulting in the inability to push their body up. They said this would eventually paralyze the pectoral and intercostal muscles, meaning inhalation was possible, but exhalation would require lifting the entire body. Without exhalation, carbon dioxide builds in the lungs and bloodstream and, spasmodically, they would be able to lift long enough to take a short breath, only prolonging the process of this ultimate form of cruelty.

That may have been the only time my mind has been truly, wonderfully blown by something produced by ATI. This only furthered my habit of sneaking medical encyclopedias into my room at night. The idea that God made the body's reflex to heal itself—to know what it needs to maintain homeostasis, when to trigger the desire for water, how it conserves circulation—I loved all of it. I loved the idea that someone could intervene when a bodily system wasn't working properly and change their fate, and I really loved the idea of knowing why each system affected the others. While my asthma attacks were terrifying, I also felt so much more calm once I knew that, even though it was a lung problem, why my heart had to get involved and start beating its ass off during the attack. I began digging through the Wisdom Booklets for more lessons like that, the ones filled with the traumatic comfort I'd begun to crave.

I read as much as I could to get ready for my medic classes but, little did I know, there would be very little overlap between ATI's books and the American Heart Association's books. We learned to look for the "reversible causes" during each assessment, meaning, "Is there something causing the distress that we are capable of fixing?" I was ready for this one and confidently wrote on my test that the cause was either a sickness unto chastisement, death, or the glory of God. Easy A. I almost got expelled until my teacher understood I was being completely serious. Although he turned out to be a villain to others later on, I'll be forever grateful that instead of kicking me out, he gave me extra assignments and allowed me to talk through a test's answers if I had erroneously let the cult seep into my thinking, actively beginning my deconstruction process and facilitating my dream of being out of the church bus and into the ambulance.

We're taught to look for the "Hs and Ts," because most of the things we can fix start with those two letters. The list is: Hypovolemia, Hypoxia, Hydrogen ion excess (acidosis), Hypoglycemia, Hypokalemia, Hyperkalemia, Hypothermia, Tension pneumothorax, Tamponade – Cardiac, Toxins, Thrombosis (pulmonary embolus), Thrombosis (myocardial infarction), and Trauma. However, my Rolodex started rattling off questions like, "Do demons fall under the toxins category?" I spewed confident answers like, "Heel bruised" (snake bite), "Temptation" (maybe someone tried to gouge out their eye), "Thorns in a crown!" and "Hematidrosis!", which is sweating blood, a very rare condition that takes place during crucifixion. Damn Wisdom Booklets were no help for CPR class!

I studied every chance I had and eventually learned how much more there was to know than the small fragments of facts hidden in the Wisdom Booklets, as if they'd been a Where's Waldo of education. I fell in love with paramedicine, thanks to my obsession with connecting crucifixion's final cause of death to suffocation, secondary to nailed hands and the positioning of their prisoner, that a traumatic (external) injury can trigger a medical (internal) crisis.

It wasn't that I enjoyed suffering; it's quite the opposite. I want to stop the suffering. I enjoy knowing the physical process of what was taking place and causing the suffering. The more I learned, the more I might be able to fix. Between caring for Grandma and the Wisdom Booklets' lessons on how to handle trauma with the stories of the Bible characters I loved, I'd learned I needed to numb myself enough to look at the injury separate from the person.

I made the mistake of looking at a woman's chipped nail polish during her organ harvesting. It made me think about how, until a few hours ago, she was a complete person, someone who picked out nail polish colors. What had she been doing when it chipped? After that, I knew I'd have to stop myself from looking at anything that made this body an individual made of anything but standard parts. I think it's why I don't find nakedness during needed care awkward at all. I can separate the body from the person.

In reading the lesson on crucifixion, I learned to turn off the feelings of deep sorrow that I put my Savior on the cross, and allowed myself to become entranced by the disease process described in the Wisdom Booklets: "A deep crushing pain deep in the chest as the pericardium slowly fills with serum and begins to compress the heart. The compressed heart is struggling to pump heavy, thick, sluggish blood into the tissues- the tortured lungs are making a frantic effort to gasp in small gulps of air. The markedly dehydrated tissues send their flood of stimuli to the brain. Jesus gasps, 'I thirst.'" I had been engrossed by the blood's consistency changes due to the compressed heart, but once it circled back to His thirst, the body became a person again. If I was going to make it, I had to keep that from happening.

* * *

I responded to a call in the middle of the night for "a car under a truck," and found a tractor trailer parked along the pull-off of a rest stop with a small car wedged almost totally under the back of it. The truck driver said he had been asleep and only felt a light tap, so maybe the damage wasn't as bad as we expected.

It was worse.

While we waited for the tow truck, the fire department was able to stabilize the vehicles, so I could crawl underneath the truck and check for survivors in the car. I was able to see there had been no secondary passengers and I could reach my arm in just far enough to check for the driver's pulse and confirm there was no air movement in his lungs.

I never, ever want to walk away from a scene only 99.9 percent sure someone was dead, only to learn later they were clinging to life and I let go for them, so I chatted with the other responders as we waited for the car to be towed out. I knew it was a tragic event but stayed disconnected enough not to be upset at the sight of a body emerging from under the truck. Once the car was out, it wasn't as horrific as we expected; it just looked like someone reclining in a convertible with their arm out the window (the car was not a convertible prior to colliding with the tractor trailer).

I walked up to the car alone, the other responders chatting and filling out paperwork a few yards away. I brought my heart monitor, in case I needed to confirm for my chart that he was pulseless, but as soon as I saw his face, I put it down. He had been decapitated, his head dangling by skin into the backseat. I shouted to the others, "It's confirmed with decapitation," and they sighed that sigh we all like to lean on for a sliver of comfort and said, "At least it was instant and they didn't know what hit them."

I stood there in the dark looking into the eyes of someone who knew a terror no one can mimic. It was excruciatingly obvious he had known exactly what was about to happen, as he had no time to stop himself from driving into a truck, when he had expected to find an empty roadway. My mind's Rolodex instantly flipped back to the moment when I read "I thirst" and my numb disconnect broke when I saw the purest expression of terror looking back at me. I learned to check pupils, but not look into their eyes. I had to learn that the process of making my dreams come true would be scattered with nightmares.

People ask when exactly I left the cult, but I don't have a true date and time. It was a slow process of being open to learning new things that eventually drew me out.

On one of my shifts not long ago, on a Sunday, I responded to a call in the area filled with the children I used to bring to Sunday school. On the way to the call, the church's red bus had to pull over to yield us the right of way. My whole world felt complete in those few seconds. I'd done it. I burst out singing Elsa's "I know I left a life behind but I'm too relieved to grieve!" It's a good thing my partners are used to my spontaneous singing by now, so they weren't fazed in the least.

I watched the church bus grow smaller in our mirror as we left it further behind. That is what leaving a cult looks like. It's not some grand explosion of burning Bibles and raiding Hot Topic; it's constantly moving forward as your captor shrinks in the distance behind you. People think I became a paramedic to save others, which is true, but becoming a paramedic is the thing that saved me.

8

Satan's Doorbell

"Doctors have discovered that the seed of the man is an alien substance to the woman. It triggers responses similar to those of an "allergic" reaction. A woman who has one husband is able to develop an "immunity" to this reaction; however, a promiscuous woman's immune system becomes confused and unable to distinguish alien substances. This confusion is a key to the development of cancer."

—Medicine Resource, Wisdom Booklet 19

I f he's even read this far, I'd say this is the chapter my father is going to want to skip. Actually, I'll encourage it, or else holidays are going to be weird.

You've reached the part of my book in which I've finally found myself smiling as I write.

I'm not sure if I have a far-above-average sex drive or if I was just made to feel that way after sex was presented to me as something that went from forbidden when you're single to a chore when you're married. It was never presented as something a female could actually enjoy.

I've been fascinated by sex and by bodies, especially my own, ever since I can remember. And I really like sex. I identify as a cis-gender pan, she/her/hers, but when fundamentalism pushed the "facts" that men think about sex every seven seconds and women only think about it when they have to, I began to wonder if something was wrong with me as a girl. I thought about sex constantly, but sex was never presented as something females enjoyed; rather, it was endured, if they couldn't find an excuse to get out of it. It was a wife's requirement to keep her husband satisfied—for, if he wasn't, he would not be able to succeed in his professional life. If someone in the church got a promotion, you knew his wife had learned a new trick.

As someone who was fascinated by sex but forbidden from learning anything factual, I decided to study my own body instead. My mirror was my best friend, which proved to be extremely beneficial when everyone was telling me everything was fine, but I knew it wasn't after noting changes in my skin. My education lacked so much that I ended up teaching myself. I became the first patient my urogynecologist ever had who could locate their own urethra without a mirror or instructions. And here you thought you'd go your whole life without encountering someone humble-bragging around their urethra.

My sex education was a compilation of purity culture scare tactics, highly inappropriate uncles, poorly cleared internet history, and whatever I could piece together from sneaking medical encyclopedias into my room late at night. I picked up a few things here and there by listening to adults talk, mostly my Gramma every time my aunt announced a pregnancy. Gramma is constantly complaining about women who don't squeeze the aspirin between their knees tightly enough to prevent more pregnancies. This led to about a decade of confusion as to why pharmacies kept all their oral birth control pills behind the counter, yet all the aspirin was out for anyone to access; and why wouldn't Hobby Lobby or Chick-Fil-A let their staff have aspirin?

I'd heard women got pregnant if they slept with a man. When I saw on the news that a bunch of people were going to camp on the beach in early Spring 1999 so they could have the first baby of the century, I was convinced beach camping was especially dangerous. Ironically proven since my surprise twins came from camping at the beach.

I definitely didn't want to have a baby when I was a kid, so I never even pretended to camp with a boy. I always made sure to keep an aspirin tucked between my knees if I was going to watch a movie on the couch with my male cousins, so if I fell asleep, I wouldn't wake up pregnant. I might have been confused but at least I was prepared.

I was fortunate enough to be one of the few amongst my friends to have a mother who at least explained the vital aspects of puberty at an early age. I would have to go into public bathroom stalls with her so, by the time I was 3 or 4, I knew that if your vagina bleeds, sometimes it means your body is old enough to have a baby and you'd have to have a giant purse to lug all those giant pads around. Pads were the only option unless you wanted to be raped by the Devil's sticks or sit on a camel's saddlebag for a week. When the oldest daughter of our family friends got her first period, they made a huge deal of it, going out to dinner with all the "women" (those who had experienced a period) amongst their family and close friends. I'd never been happier not to have had my period in my life. I was that strange girl who couldn't wait to get her period, and I kind of still enjoy having it, but I did not want to go to dinner to celebrate my friend's newly shed uterine lining with her great-grandma.

I wasn't shy about asking questions, but I didn't always know what to ask. My mother would always reply with the shortest, most factual answer she could, to get me to stop asking. When I was 7 and had a baby sister, I asked how babies are made. She told me about how sperm swim their way to an egg when it's on its way to being a period and, if one works its way in, it becomes a baby. I thought I was the fucking coolest kid in our entire double-wide trailer church. I told one friend the information I'd uncovered but swore her to secrecy because I knew we weren't supposed to talk about our sinful body parts. She thanked me for that lesson as she was shooting the photos for this cover.

When I was 3, I asked my mother how a baby fits out of a vagina. She said, "It stretches to let the baby out." Well. That sent me down a large spiral of assumptive panic about my chances of motherhood, so I decided to do the only logical thing: stretching exercises. I sat on my welcome-mat-sized Beauty and the Beast rug next to my bed and lined up my dolls from Polly Pocket to "Big Dolly," a life-sized infant doll, to see which dolls' heads I'd be able to fit. Polly Pocket started me off on a high of confidence since she was no problem. I made it as far as the Playskool dollhouse baby before becoming terrified that I literally wasn't cut out to be a mother. So, every night, I stretched. I did end up getting a few small tears, but I thought those few drops were my period; I was thrilled with this extra level of progress, especially since I was obsessed with getting my period and this put me about nine years ahead of the average girl. My mother eventually caught me "exercising" one night and told me to stop because I'd break something and never be able to have kids, which was the only threat I needed. She said everything stays tiny until the baby is actually born, so "stop pulling on it." I traded my exercises for fervent checks in my handheld kitty mirror. The tail was the perfect length handle to see everything just right and monitor any changes.

I decided it must grow slowly on its own because I'd heard Gramma have some vivid conversations while holding a giant kielbasa. So, I knew there was somehow more stretching than people were letting on, but I hadn't yet made the connection that the kielbasa was the uterus' magic wand nor that it was meant to represent a penis. I didn't even figure penises were part of the process.

I'd only ever seen one for a few seconds when I, the most uptight 5-year-old ever to exist, had insisted the neighbors prove they weren't wearing their wet bathing suits on my swing set. I have never been one to take someone's word on something so, in his efforts to get me to share my swings, Liz's 3-year-old brother pulled his shorts open in front to show me he'd taken off his suit. I was in shock at what I saw. Didn't something like that get in the way? Wasn't that... thing... uncomfortable? Is that why guys had that bump in their pants? Did they roll it up like a snail to keep it in place? It was unfortunately awkward to have all these questions at the same time I was eye-level to most pelvises. I'd have to wait another 13 years for the answers.

A few years later, when I was 8 or 9, I was playing in my grandma's backyard in my purple 101 Dalmatians bathing suit, taking breaks every so often to cool off in the tiny kiddie pool she'd gotten at the grocery store. Later that night, I was back at home, diligently checking my mirror, and noticed a small black dot next to my right labia. I knew it was a tick, and because I lived in Connecticut, the place Lyme disease was first described, I knew how to remove it safely without bothering anyone else. I brought cotton swabs, peroxide, and tweezers into my room, which was actually the dining room of our one-bedroom apartment that my parents had turned into my room by hanging curtains in the two double-wide doorways, one leading to the kitchen and one to the living room. Using my American Girl buttons, I pinned together the cloth curtains known to blow open if someone opened the refrigerator and got to work. My father looked through the curtains anyway and I was immediately punished. I had no idea why I was being punished for trying to perform a life-saving procedure that my parents had trained me to do. I didn't understand he was punishing me for what he assumed was self-gratification; I had no idea orgasms or masturbation even existed. I figured it was more of an if-God-wants-you-to-die-let-it-happen situation. But I was doing pretty ok mentally at the time and didn't exactly feel like dying, so I waited until I knew he was asleep and removed the tick later that night, bitterly angry that I'd been punished for doing something to protect myself.

Before ATI brought about surprise Spiritual cleanses, we had a few movies that depicted unmarried kisses. My all-time favorite scene was "16 Going On 17" and I was on a mission to have my first kiss take place in a gazebo in the rain, not caring that my pink dress was going to get soaked. I'm sure I'd only practiced this scene eight thousand times before my father told me, "If you kiss someone on the lips, that means you're married, and divorce is against the Ten Commandments, so you'll be married forever." Several of my friends had also been told this and we simply accepted it as complete truth, especially since a kiss was such a big deal at a wedding.

When I was 5, I was fellowshipping with a boy my age while our moms had tea. It was a play-date, but we weren't allowed to use that sinful term created by The World, and "play-courtship" didn't really roll off the tongue. This boy's father literally wrote the book on courtship versus dating. He and I started playing Simon Says and it led to, "Simon says kiss my cheek," "Kiss my hand." We got all the way to chin before we decided we should stop. He said, "If we keep playing, I'm going to say lips next," which we both believed would mean we were married. I remember feeling so grown up and excited, not because it was forbidden, but because I liked him and liked kissing each other's faces. I thought about what we both believed to be his proposal, seriously considering it because he was a preacher boy and that meant I'd be guaranteed a role as a Sunday school teacher. But, eventually, we decided against our kiss because we lived in different states and didn't talk on the phone much, so we probably shouldn't get married. That was the last time we ever saw each other.

I ended up being incredibly relieved I hadn't married him because, two years later, I met The Boy With The Chickens, who I truly believed I was going to marry. By this time, I was fully obsessed with Laura Ingalls so, when I met a boy who lived on a farm, I was smitten. (He didn't really live on a farm. He had goats, chickens, and a garden but, to my Spam-and-Spaghetti-O-nourished mind, he was a farmer.) He was one of half a dozen siblings and I loved his family. We met at the same double-wide church where I'd corrupted Megan with the knowledge of biology earlier that year, a church founded by one of ATI's original families. The entire church homeschooled and most members were in ATI. Being accepted into ATI is a long process. Both of our families were accepted when we were 9, which meant we would both be going to Knoxville—our first trip together! Things were obviously getting pretty serious.

Our families were assigned to the same dorm and we would make sure our families always left for the sessions at the same time, so we could sit a row apart on the conference bus. On the bus ride back, I would still have a neatly enhanced countenance and perfect flow to my skirt, while he would be sunburned, scraped, and filthy. I lived for the end of the day, when I could escape the monotony of Pre-Excel and hear all about his adventures at ALERT cadets. One day, he said he would take me away from the world of perfection and teach me to rappel, but that was back when we were innocent children and believed we'd have more autonomy as we aged. Each year, I'd leave Knoxville exhausted and depressed by the idea of only seeing him weekly, not daily.

The Boy With The Chickens and I spent five years never openly proclaiming our love for one another, but secretly enjoying our flirtatious young courtship. I started sewing my dresses so the skirts would be as puffy as possible, with lots of extra fabric to drape over our hands, as we clasped them between us throughout the 45-minute sermons. It wasn't long before we held hands with our fingers interlaced—still under the puff of my dress, of course. Hand-holding with interlaced fingers was something in which only the extremely progressive, committed couples indulged. On hymn-sing nights, we would request the most unpopular hymns we could find, so everyone in church would need to look at the words. Since we were the same height, we would get to share a hymnal—an extremely intimate act. Men never shared a hymnal with another man, nor anyone who wasn't his wife. Women could share with other women and children. For us to have our hands on the same book, our faces close enough together to both see the words, that was my rainy-gazebo-kiss moment.

My pocket-sized purple diary with the tiny pink hearts and lock that didn't work is filled with pages upon pages of my name written next to his last name. My family would go to his house often and, even though I never wanted to hold his chicken, he did teach me how to milk his goat. That was a completely literal sentence; I'm not about to use an inuendo about a couple of 8-year-olds. During one visit, he took me under the porch where they slaughtered the chickens and gave me a sunflower-shaped cloth barrette he'd found. In my eyes, it was a diamond ring. I wore it almost every day and kept it in the center of my dresser, not on the braided yarn with the rest of the bows. I still have it with my jewelry.

* * *

The entirety of ATI's sex education was "no." All we ever learned was we weren't allowed to touch someone of the opposite sex until marriage. Promiscuity caused cervical cancer. All blow jobs caused throat cancer. Our virginity and potential loss of such was often compared to perfect flowers with the petals viciously torn off, chewed and spit out candy bars, new cars with immediately lost value once driven off the lot, or white gowns with red dye thrown at them. In the Basic, I'd learned Bill could spot who was a virgin and who was not; virgins had a joyful light in their eyes that turned to clouded rebellion once they allowed themselves to be defiled—much like when Adam and Eve became aware of evil after eating the forbidden fruit. There was a special exception if someone experienced sexual assault, but only if it was determined through counseling with their father and pastor that the victim played no role in the temptation using ATI's chart on counseling sexual assault.

Before the light can return to our eyes, we are instructed to find gratitude towards the abuser for allowing us to become mighty in Spirit and strengthening our relationship with God. I wanted to have all those wonderful characteristics! I'd seen this chart and heard this sermon so many times, I spent most of my tween and teen years wondering why God didn't love me enough to have someone rape me. That thinking error followed me through my 20s and took a significant amount of therapy to deconstruct.

* * *

Depending on how liberal the standards of each family were, some would agree that once a couple entered a courtship, they could hold hands. If you saw a couple greet each other with a side-hug, you could safely assume they were engaged. My cohorts took these standards very seriously. At one seminar, a girl slipped and got hurt. The closest person to her was a man, and she would not let him help her up because she had vowed not to be touched by a man until marriage. I had proclaimed no such vows, but since even accidentally bumping into someone of the opposite sex was seen as defilement; being in the apprenticeship choir with only an armrest between us felt like the equivalent of every song about that euphoric rush of young, rebellious affection that comes with making love in the green grass behind the stadium.

When I was 16, my parents agreed to let me volunteer as a candy striper at the community hospital down the hill, and, in the corniest pun ever, it was all downhill from there. Little did I know, I'd be sitting next to the guy with whom I would share my first kiss, and our orientation would be led by Brandon, the most competent 16-year-old on Earth. (He was kind enough to let me use his name in the book.)

No one quite knew what to make of me, since I wore flowing, floor-length khaki skirts and wouldn't ride the elevators with boys. Despite my being the weird girl, Brandon started to like-like me and I have the diary entries and handwritten cards to prove it. When he first started to flirt with me, he typed out the lyrics to "Don't Want to Miss a Thing" and put it in the pocket of my red-and-white striped apron. I was blown away and thought he had written it. He could have taken the credit and I wouldn't have found out until years later, but he didn't. I imagine this type of innocence in a love interest is only fun for so long. Most reasonable people want their partner to be an equal, not someone who is constantly discovering the world around them as if they'd been kept in an underground bunker and requires perpetual social orientation (both men I married can attest to this). Brandon was the one I would go to with my endless questions about this world I was just discovering, and he patiently transitioned from running my Candy Striper orientation to orientation of the world around me.

I believe he was the first true gentleman I'd ever experienced. Sure, the ATI guys stayed far away, but that was due to rules, not personal respect. Of course, being surrounded by average teenagers meant full immersion into a world of hormones and sex drives, for which I was not prepared. When I finally had the nerve to ask what it was all our friends were talking about and why it was such a big deal, he handled it beautifully. Instead of taking full advantage by creating a hands-on learning experience, he did the most respectable, helpful thing he could do. He brought me his textbooks from school and ended up giving me what I imagine was a full sex-ed class. I spent a lot of time saying, "Noooooo. Are you sure?"

For the first time in my life, someone had managed to present sex in a way that seemed healthy and fun. So much of what he explained was completely new information to me. Everything he told me about sounded like an opportunity for mutual pleasure. Instead of sex being this horridly forbidden concept that would suddenly become my job after I said "I do," it became something no longer terrifying to consider. It finally dawned on me that what happened to my body was my choice. If I was going to hold off, I was going to do so because I wanted to, not because I wanted to avoid Spiritual cataracts.

Later that year, Brandon asked me to be his prom date. I felt like the chance to have a normal coming-of-age experience was finally just within my reach. I knew my father would never approve, so I wasn't even going to bother to ask. My mom, on the other hand, would surely jump at the chance to be the Fairy Godmother of this story after spanking all those pillows for me. I knew I'd never grab books from my locker, walk into the wrong class, or have my personality defined by where I sat in the cafeteria, but I thought if I could just go to a prom, if I could live the fantasy that is "Barry Is Going To Prom," I'd be able to taste a moment of normalcy. I just wanted the one night that, for everyone else, would be unmatched for glamor and excitement until their wedding. But, alas, no amount of pleading got her to say "yes."

I had dreamed of going to prom ever since learning they existed. I watched as a group of girls got ready for theirs next door with Liz. I helped with their hair and took all the photos of them with their dates and families. I was in one of the photos. I was finally wearing jeans, but everyone else had a gown. When I had pictured my Cinderella moment, I hadn't pictured the version where Cinderella is left behind in her rags. I watched as they climbed into the limo and toasted glasses of ginger ale as they drove away, leaving me in the driveway with all of their parents, who didn't really know what to say to me. I comforted myself with the fact that I'd been asked to four proms and some girls who go to school aren't even asked at all—which, in hindsight, is pretty bitchy.

The closest I'd ever get as a teenager was the dinner the hospital hosted for the volunteers each year. Since I hadn't been able to go to prom with Brandon, he asked me to be his date for the hospital's event. My parents agreed to let me go, but with my core group of friends, not as anyone's date. They could call it whatever they wanted; all I needed was that "yes." I began sewing my gown immediately. It never crossed my mind to buy a dress—ever—nor to ask literally anyone what the expected attire would be. My gown was bubble gum pink with sparkles and had a huge skirt that made me look like I was floating. The pattern was for a sleeveless gown but I had to compromise and put sheer, short sleeves on it.

I've never received more compliments on a dress in my life, which I believe was because I was the only one in a gown. Everyone was dressed nicely, but in much more of a cocktail-hour look than I had decided to don. I was used to being unlike anyone else. While missing out bothered me, standing out was kind of my jam; so, I decided at that moment that I'd always rather be overdressed than underdressed.

As the event was coming to an end, Brandon took my hand, brought me to an open area of the room, and asked me to dance. He said he knew I'd missed out on everything else and he was going to do his best to give me a normal experience. We danced to no music, everyone watching and likely thinking we were idiots who had no idea what this event was actually supposed to be. I give him a lot of credit—that was probably extremely embarrassing for him, but he did it with a smile. He could have easily pressed his advantage with the girl who relied on him for all the knowledge needed to make it through being 17. But that night ended with one kiss. That was it. Just one single, mint-flavored moment with a trumpet player, in which to cram all my missed high school experiences.

My father's plan was for me to enter a courtship with a man of his choosing. There was only ever one guy from church who asked my father to enter a courtship with me (and I had no idea at the time). This guy had never spoken to me, aside from asking about my soul-winning numbers or if I'd washed the baptismal clothes yet. Not once had we ever engaged in a personal conversation, yet entering an engaged-to-be-engaged relationship was the next fundamentalist step toward determining if we should spend our lives together.

I was relieved to learn my father had told him no, but couldn't figure out why he'd said no. My father likes that guy a lot. My father got him a job. They exchange casual emails about their lives. My father told me what he assumed was the obvious reason for his denial: the guy was Black.

I wanted to puke when I heard that. I'd always known my family was racist, but we had friends who were interracial couples, so it hadn't occurred to me that someone would be denied solely because of their skin color. I'd soon learn that many fundamentalists believe the story of the tower of Babel is a warning against interracial mingling. The denial and outright hatred of interracial relationships became more apparent as friends tried to pursue similar relationships only to be denied for the same reasons. The guys who would gravitate toward me at Pastor's

School and Youth Conference were detestable, but they got to sit near me because they were White.

That was when I knew I'd never be able to leave my relationship choices to someone else. How could someone possibly make an accurate recommendation for a partner when they wouldn't look past an "unchangeable"? I didn't go on to make great choices by any means, but I was determined not to let race be a deciding factor. As time went on, the acceptance broadened and my sister did end up marrying interracially - and our father loves him.

Since I wasn't about to play by the courtship rules, I hid most of my romantic life from everyone but my "worldly" friends. When I was 18, I had my very first official boyfriend. He was extremely patient with me and my confliction over what was my boundary versus the church's. I'd signed a contract with the church, promising I wouldn't kiss until marriage (I'd signed it after that one kiss with the trumpet player) so, for the first two months we dated, we never kissed and he never pressured me. I slept over at his apartment, but we stuck to holding hands and keeping our jam jams on. When I eventually tell my kids "Yeah, well I remember how I acted when I was your age", it won't mean the same as when most parents say it.

To keep myself awake during the 45 minutes of being screamed at during sermons three times a week, I'd save up thoughts I wanted to ponder without being bothered; I spent several sermons' worth of time pondering my purity contract and how I really felt about it. At first, I'd repress any feelings of physical desire, figuring they were sent directly from Satan. I wasn't about to let anyone, including myself, ring his doorbell and pave the way down the slippery slope to my sin cave. The doorbell is my clitoris (read as Nathan Fillion's Captain Hammer).

I came to the conclusion that I was at a critical point in my choose-your-own-adventure story. I could stick to the contract that wasn't even notarized and spend my entire life without the memory of young love. Sure, purity culture's aim is to prevent heartbreak—but it also prevents the joyous split-second rush that only comes with potentially making your own mistakes. Purity culture took away any of my choose-your-own-adventure auton-omy and, yes, there are tons of people who regret not waiting, but there are also many who don't.

I sat up straight in my family's usual fourth-row-from-the-front pew and, much like a parent who sleeps through a thun-derstorm but wakes instantly at the slight whimper of their child, I tuned out all the preacher's words that weren't Bible references, so I could robotically follow along as I'd practiced in my years of Sword drills, while I figured out how I felt about premarital kissing. Spoiler alert: I landed on Team Kissing.

My first boyfriend was very sweet about my decision and repeatedly asked if I was sure, because he didn't want me to regret anything. I don't. After I kissed him, I realized two things. The first: kissing is really, really fun, as long as the other person decently matches my style. And the second: nothing about who I was changed because I'd smushed my face against the face of a fellow candy striper, repeatedly and frequently. He broke up with me about a month later, which devastated me. But, really, I don't blame him at all. Dating me as I climbed out of the cult was a lot more work than any 18-year-old should have to deal with.

Later that year, I stopped suppressing the crush I was devel-oping on one of the guys I worked with when we were both baby EMTs. He played Harold Hill in his high school play so, you know, how could I not swoon over his convincing stance on sadder-but-wiser girls? One morning, as we were heading to our cars after spending our entire overnight shift talking, inches apart in our ambulance, as I lay on the stretcher and he lay on the bench seat, I mustered up enough courage and told him I wanted to kiss him. You know what happened next? Not so much as a "kiss my foot or have an apple." In what may have been my most humbling teen experience, he gave me a high five. About a decade later, our careers crossed again and we finally made up for lost time—although, he didn't find my offer of a high five after we were done as hilarious as I did.

And, yes, I stopped writing this chapter specifically to send him every GIF of Amy and Seth high fiving that I could find.

* * *

By the time it was winter, I'd met Mustache and, after a few 140-character-limit text exchanges, he took me with him to put flowers on his friend's grave. Allegedly, the previous night when he was holding the trauma shears she had given him, she sent him a sign that he should date me, so he asked me to be his girlfriend. As word of our relationship got around, one day as Brandon and I were running 911s together, Brandon asked me why I had agreed to be Mustache's girlfriend.

I thought about my answer carefully, because I knew he was asking out of genuine curiosity and not jealousy. Mustache and I had very little in common outside of being EMTs and he wasn't exactly known as the world's kindest person. The truth is I wasn't really sure why I had said yes. I had crushes on much more attractive and gentlemanly guys, but I was someone who had been kissed—a "backslidden harlot," as I'd been told—so I felt I'd need to set my sights on guys with lower standards. My answer disappointed me as much as it did Brandon when I replied, "Well, he asked." I'd spent so much of my life hearing that all my value would be lost if I wasn't completely naive to pleasure and I'd have to be grateful to have anyone want me; I'd just spoken it into existence.

I told Brandon I assumed Mustache and I would break up after a few weeks. That was my plan. But I'd never broken up with anyone for any reason other than "My parents said no," so, I sort of didn't get around to it until four years later. I really loved his family and loved our group of friends. Plus, if I broke up with him, I'd also be trading all the carefree fun for awkward tension. So, I spent years convincing myself I was happy. This meant also keeping him happy enough to not hit me with the metal runform box or hold knives to my throat as a crazy trust exercise.

Even though I'd been happy with my choice to dismiss any purity culture rules about kissing, I was still holding out on sex itself, which I only defined as vaginal, since that was the only type I'd read about in the medical books. I was still convinced the light switch for my Spiritually bright eyeballs was tucked deep inside and would immediately be switched off by any hint of a penis. A popular way around this is what we Exers have deemed "God's Loophole" (Garfunkel and Oates' song may appear as satire but, I assure you, it wasn't for my crowd); since preaching had only ever condoned the act of sodomy between same-sex couples, girls could technically offer the same route of entry without ever admitting patrons to their sin cave. I hated it but it kept him happy. Plus, he often mentioned that being behind me was a great option since it meant he didn't have to see my pimple-covered face. Hey, if I wasn't beautiful, at least I was fun, right?

The morning after we'd first utilized the loophole, my mother woke up all upset over having a dream about what took place. While I don't believe in psychics, my mother has some level of creepy ability to know exactly what I've been up to. She still does it. Frequently, when I'm about to call her, I wait a few minutes and, usually, she ends up calling me. I don't know how she does it, but it's weird and it's convinced me never to lie to her; if I've learned anything from Disney, it's that you don't lie to characters with magical abilities. Eventually, her nightmares of promiscuity faded into her telling me she would know what I was up to that weekend by whether or not I'd put my "recreational underwear" in the laundry. I think that was the pivotal point of our relationship when I knew I could include her in my life. She wasn't about to help me and if I got caught by the church, I'd be on my own. But, as long as I was honest with her, she didn't give me shit for the choices, which made her the most liberal ATI mom I knew.

I figured that since sex was painful for me and only fun for him, I was doing it right, according to every ladies' breakout session I'd been to. Growing up during the Clinton impeachment had allowed me to catch bits of news stories in waiting rooms or tabloids at Stop & Shop, and eavesdrop my way into a sexual revolution. I'd overheard coworkers argue over whether or not it was "actually sex." Even though Bill (Gothard, not Clinton) taught us it was the cause of throat cancer, I decided to explore my other options and asked the only sexually active girl I trusted if she would teach me how to give a blow job. She blushed a bit, but I will forever see her as an unsung hero of my life who didn't shed one iota of judgment over my inquisition for a consenting (18+) act. Working alongside each other, we dutifully stacked the used hospital commodes onto a cart, while she not only explained that there's usually no actual blowing involved, but also that I could enjoy what I was doing. Girls could enjoy sex for reasons other than making the man a success? I'd gone to her hoping she'd teach me to open my jaws—what she really taught me was how to open a whole new world. If you're one of the cameos in this chapter, you owe her a debt of gratitude.

Between the lifetime of beliefs shoved deeper than my current IUD and the endless movies, songs, and books romanticizing a virgin's first time, I'd set my vaginal virginity on an unwavering pedestal. That was my line and no one was going to make me cross it. Honestly, I'd always felt like each new line I crossed was done in my own time—for me and no one else—but, if that was the case, I should be getting something out of it.

One Wednesday night after church, we sat in the back of his car in the tiny parking lot of a 9-to-5 business, talking and eventually stumbling toward our own paradise by the dashboard lights. That song was always the one I'd be pulled onto the dance floor to duet because everyone pegged me as the girl who was holding out. Have you ever noticed how accurately that song depicts the damaging potential of purity culture? They were so convinced they'd have to be married if they slept together, that they spent their entire lives committed to someone who made them miserable. No one ever taught them it's possible for something to be right in that moment but not forever. At the time, I loved him enough—not for who he was but because he was someone who still wanted me, even though I'd been kissed.

No, make that even though I'd kissed someone. I'm taking credit for the wonderful things that happened. As much as they'd like to think it false, girls can be the ones who make the unregretful choice to be active. I wasn't a stationary stumbling block, as they'd always portrayed me. I was an active participant in the glorious, consensual ritual of making out. I decided my virginity wasn't something I owed him or anyone. His willingness to date me wasn't some heroically valiant act on his part, to swoop in as if he was that creep who first pursued Daphne Bridgerton. I didn't become weak because the idea of pleasure was all I wanted in that moment.

Hearing the world around me as my personal soundtrack meant I had the end of that song playing on a loop in my head and, even though I figured we'd be married eventually, I didn't use that thought to justify sleeping with him. I decided this was something I wanted to do because it was right for who I was in that moment. I wasn't going to let my vagina's guest list be the determining factor for who I married. I felt powerful, like I was in control of something for the first time in my life.

I bunched up my pink floral skirt that matched the one the pastor's wife had, climbed over him, and announced I was ready to do this. Four minutes later, I was the same person I'd been that morning. As soon as it was over, I looked in the mirror to check how dim my eyes had become. Shockingly, they looked exactly the same.

I was almost disappointed by how little anything had changed. All my life, I'd been told my entire worth as a person rode on who I rode; I was annoyed at how much energy I'd wasted on a standard I didn't make for myself. I began to think something was wrong with me because I didn't feel like I was giving away pieces of my heart and, I was enjoying myself. I became quite skilled at separating sex and emotions, to the extent that I cringe when I hear the phrase "make love." It makes me feel icky just typing that. I've had a lot of sex and I've been married twice, but I don't think I've ever "made love" and I'm not bothered by that. Sex isn't emotional for me. I can't help wondering if it would have been if I'd had realistic expectations from the beginning.

After Mustache and I broke up, it hit me that I would be someone who had a list of more than one sexual partner. While it was a weird concept to process, it was also incredibly freeing to know I could filter out any guy who saw my personal choices as a reason to devalue me.

Deciding to sleep with the second person was actually a more difficult choice than the first. At least with Mustache, I could tell myself I'd only ever be with one person because we could get married. Once I'd slept with someone else, that would be it. I'd be someone who slept with "people" instead of "a person"; that was a lot to swallow. (That was not an intentional pun, but I'm leaving it. This book is an emotional rollercoaster. I think we could all use a really cheap joke right about now.) But after four years of Mustache, I was excited to sleep with someone who was actually excited about being with me and not just a warm hole.

It was a completely different and wonderful experience. When I made the choice to sleep with him, I never in a million years thought we would get married. But we did. And the sex was so great, we managed to squeeze in one last romp while waiting for our divorce to be finalized.

Making the choice to sleep with Dreamy Eyes, my current husband was the easiest choice I've ever made. Our arrangement was the exact opposite of purity culture standards. Neither of us wanted to date the other, but we wanted orgasms without the hassle of feelings. I think we nailed it for a really long time.

I spent my next few years single years making up for lost time. I didn't ever feel like the backslidden harlot other people saw. I felt powerful, never slutty. I felt equal to men, especially when I was able to feel comfortable running into someone in a social setting after having given them detailed instructions on how they should be ringing my doorbell or how loudly they should say my name. I like that about myself. I like that I don't feel awkwardly vulnerable just because we shared a naked hobby for a while. I've never taken a walk of shame; I prefer a strut of pride. There are people I would never choose to revisit, but there are none I regret. I love that I was able to experience a variety of personalities, places, genders, styles, and plenty of guys from Tinder who acted like real loopholes. Now I've transitioned to SNL's depiction of Zillow being the fantasy app of my 30s, and my best seductive line is, "Ok, but tonight, don't forget to fuck me, ok? Because I took a night shower and I don't want to waste it." I'm very comfortable with the path I've taken. I know if I'd followed their rules and my hypothetical husband and I had only ever experienced each other, I would have always wondered "What if?"

But that's me. That doesn't mean I believe everyone should do it my way. I don't believe there is one right way to go about one's sexuality. If a person wants to wait until their wedding night, I fully support them in that, as long as it's their choice, not an expectation. If they don't want to wait, that's their choice; no one else should expect to make it for them.

I'm not a chewed candy bar. I'm not a stained gown. I'm a person whose value in this world is never going to change based on what I decide to do with my vagina.

9

Scream Really Loud

"This world is not my home, I'm just a-passing through. If Heaven's not my home, then Lord, what will I do? The angels beckon me to Heaven's open door and I can't feel at home in this world anymore. Oh Lord, you know I have no friend like you. If Heaven's not my home, then Lord, what will I do? The angels beckon me to Heaven's open door and I can't feel at home in this world anymore."

—The hymn that inspired my suicide attempts.

My mother tells me that when I was a baby, I would get so upset that I would hold my breath and faint. She says she became used to giving me a few rescue breaths with this routine and eventually learned that if she could get me to focus on screaming, I would get past the initial phase of holding my breath and would be fine. She says she used to have strangers stare at her for being the only parent in a public place instructing their child to "Scream, really loud!"

Even now when I'm at work, parents wonder why I'm not more concerned about their crying child; silent kids are much more worrisome. When kids are crying, they are still doing semi-ok. Of course, I want the child to be as comforted as possible but, just as my mother had learned, crying means breathing.

If I hear a child scream after being injured, I'm always slightly relieved because I know at least they are conscious and have an airway. It's the kids who fall down and don't react that send my heart plummeting. Teaching me to "scream, really loud" may be the most valuable thing my mother ever taught me, but I should have taken the advice much sooner.

Every lesson I've ever heard in a fundamentalist setting taught me that any sort of illness that could not be measured with lab results was not a real illness. ADD was for kids who needed more discipline. Depression was for people who let the devil speak louder than God.

I knew a woman at church who had anxiety attacks. I would watch as she spiraled into full panic and then talk herself back down by braiding her hair. I was in awe of her ability to acknowledge her fears as real and then use a healthy method to return to calm, rather than attempt to dismiss her thoughts as "crazy" and try to stifle what was happening. That church had "children's church" during the regular service, but I was never allowed to go because "God can use a sermon to speak to all ages, even 5-year-olds." So, I sat with my parents and listened while I watched panic turn to braids.

Ever since then, I'd find myself in a spiral of true paralyzing panic over what I'd heard in the sermons and wished I could braid my way back to calm. I'd wake up screaming from nightmares and my mother would have to talk me down. I wish this had been a silly childhood fear, but these panic spirals have been happening for 27 years and have only gotten worse. I still text my mother and make her do this now; she's the only one who can get me out of it. This might be the only part of this book where I'll leave out specifics because I'm still not ready to hear what anyone has to say about my Biblical nightmares. Even typing this has made me tachycardic.

I didn't know what was happening at the time, but I remember when I was about 5, I felt true depression for the first time. I grew up eating Spam and SpaghettiOs, so nutrition was unheard of. One day, my mother bought oatmeal, with all these wonderful health promises on the box. It was the first time I connected food with health. I quickly went from excited about learning that long-term nutrition could be the difference between life and death to a spiral of never wanting to see that oatmeal again. What was the point of prolonging my life so that I could increase my chances of outliving people I loved?! If we're all going to die anyway, why bother? Why eat things that increase energy when sleep was a far more enjoyable experience than being awake?

I've thought a lot about becoming a nutritionist once the twins start school, and one of my friends told me, "Nutritionists don't order Domino's at 2 a.m." Probably true—I bet they order around dinnertime. But that conversation made me realize that when I do that, I'm repeating the same comfort habit I learned as a kid. While it's not an extreme, immediate self-harm behavior, it's my default way of manifesting my inability to see past tomorrow.

No one in my family believed in "minor" mental illnesses. We only acknowledged the "big" ones, like being possessed, because that was covered in the Bible. Eventually, we acknowledged Dissociative Identity Disorder (DID) after watching a church member's host "switch" underwater, mid-Baptism, suddenly believing the preacher was attempting to murder him. But we didn't have any mental health concerns in our family.

Long before ATI, half my family took to silence, denial, and alcohol as an alternative to processing grief or managing conflict. No matter the issue, we all just shut up and sipped our tea. That worked for decades until the year everyone snapped and I found myself taping together torn-up letters of repudiation and keeping a list of who was disowning whom and why. Changing wills became almost habitual.

I'm still working through my own self-awareness and examining why it's relatively easy for me to cut someone out of my life who was once close. From both sides of my family, I've never known a holiday, wedding, or funeral that didn't need a rotating schedule or a distanced seating chart, so that one set of people could leave before the disowned set arrived. As far as I know, I've only been disowned—so far—by one maternal uncle, who, at one time was my biggest fan, but stopped speaking to me the day I told him I was pregnant with the twins.

Those who didn't utilize silence and denial resorted to almost the opposite behaviors. I don't even know how many doors have been replaced or wall holes were repaired at Gramma's house. Yelling was normal. I have one cousin who has the most soft, gentle voice, and we never heard her because she never yelled. Storming out with the intent of divorce was the way to end every marital conflict. I kept a bag packed and ready at all times; in case my mother decided to leave, I would be ready to go with her. Seeing as none of us knew how to have a calm, healthy discussion, most criticism—even minor—was met with, "Well, I might as well just kill myself."

No matter the issue at hand—be it backseat driving or sewing the cat's head on crooked—Gramma showed us if you were given even constructive criticism, the response was never to change the behavior or go to the vet; it was only to stop living. I heard "I'll just kill/shoot/poison/hang/bake/drown myself" so often, it became merely an expression in my family. That was what people said when they were frustrated and, to my knowledge, no one in the previous generations of my family had ever actively attempted suicide or had serious thoughts of harming themselves. (Though, recently, my elderly, distant cousin took his own life. But only after murdering his ex-wife, being charged with embezzlement, and hosting a several-hour-long potential hostage situation standoff with every special forces unit in the region. It was a whole thing.)

Becoming a mandated reporter was a massive internal struggle for me because, once I became an EMT, any mention of self-harm meant I was required to report it. I'd ask in class how to evaluate if someone truly meant it or not and, at 16, I learned the shocking news that suicidal statements aren't something we get to decide to believe or not. They all need to be taken seriously.

This frustrates Gramma constantly and she gets stuck in a loop of, "Well, I can't say anything in front of Heather without getting in trouble. I might as well just be dead." So close, Gramma. I'm the first grandchild to have kids, so I'm also her biggest censor. I would never disown Gramma, but I've had to explain that if she talks about killing herself, I can't have the twins around her. It's a vicious cycle that my cousin and I are determined to break.

My family didn't recognize that normalizing suicide almost killed me. They all knew no one meant it, but how do you make that distinction when you're a child? I knew what suicide was and I figured no one in my family had gone through with it because they simply changed their mind or had too much to do and never got around to it. I never realized suicide was harmful. I only knew it as a solution to feeling hurt.

My first suicide attempt was in January 1995. I was 6 years old.

My mother was in the hospital for an extended period of time while waiting to give birth to my sister. I knew she had come close to death during my birth and many of the complications were repeating. She knew having another baby held a great risk of killing her, but ATI taught women they were acting in sheer disobedience by limiting their family size. She was made to take on the "If I die, I die" attitude of Esther, and dutifully conceived my sister. No one had cell phones then. I clung to a beeper loaned to me by a Sunday school teacher, waiting to hear any kind of news. I was staying at my paternal grandmother's house, along with my cousin who was living there during college. My grandma cared for me well and, 10 years later, I moved back in to care for her but, nevertheless, that stay was miserable. Seeing as I was homeschooled out of separation anxiety, it should come as no shock that I had a few attachment issues of my own.

At night, my cousin would read me "James and the Giant Peach." The only thing I remember from that story is that the parents die. I heard nothing else she read after that. I was overwhelmed by the thought of my mother dying, my new sister dying, and having to live on my own with my father or grandmother. I didn't want to tell anyone I was worried. It might make my grandma think I didn't appreciate her, which I did, and it would probably make my father angry. If my mother wasn't there, who would stop me from getting hit with the wooden spoon as much as had been planned? Who would talk me out of my sermon spirals? Where would my entire world go? And that's when the hymn you read at the beginning of this chapter moved into my brain, rent free.

Although my family normalized suicide as a solution, their flippantly suggested methods didn't fit my thoroughly contemplated preferences. I didn't have access to a gun (if I had, I would have died that night) and didn't want to drown because I hate having my head under water and I didn't want my last feeling to be one of annoyance. I thought about using my asthma and running around long enough to induce a severe attack, but I was afraid to run outside in the dark, thinking someone might notice and save me. I couldn't tie a strong enough knot to something above me, so I couldn't hang.

So, one night I snuck out to the garage with my favorite blanket, the one with the satin edge my mother had replaced dozens of times, that I kept in my emergency divorce suitcase. I'd never slept without it and I wanted the last thing I'd feel to be the comfort of its satin edge. I sat in the back seat of the car and waited. I knew one of the older kids at church had taken his life by falling asleep in the car in the garage and I decided to follow suit. Thankfully, I didn't know the car needed to be on. I don't know how long I was there. I remember trying to go to sleep but being too excited to get to Heaven to drift off.

I've never been afraid of death. I attribute that to what I'd learned in church. Funerals weren't sad; they were celebrations of someone's "home-going." I'd learned to idolize death and martyrdom, reinforced by watching ATI corner my mother into a high-risk pregnancy, and it made no sense to me to hang around on earth, a place filled with suffering, when there was a much better option waiting for me after I took my last breath. I remember thinking: I believed in Jesus dying for my sins so, if I could just die, I would be there to meet my mom in Heaven and everything would be perfect. (Except for the bees. I always wondered how Heaven managed bee stings. Seeing as there's a river of honey, there must be bees everywhere. Maybe spiritual bees don't sting?)

Eventually, I cried myself to sleep but nothing happened. I stayed alive. I woke up cold and uncomfortable. I went back inside, curled up in my Lamb Chop tent and read Mother Goose all night (ok, probably 'til 11, but it felt like all night).

The thing I couldn't get out of my mind was: why didn't anyone find me? I was 6. Did they look for me? No one seemed to notice when I came back inside. No one seemed relieved to have found me. No one asked what I was doing. This whole event was probably a dreamlike timeline, when it feels like an eternity but, in reality, only a few seconds had passed. The feeling that no one would look for me only exacerbated the feeling of acting on my darkest thoughts that no one but my mother cared if I was around, and the rest of them could have fun celebrating my home-going.

My mom and sister both came home a few days later, healthy and with only a few complications. I became unfairly overprotective of my sister because I needed someone else to need me. I didn't tell anyone about my attempt. I didn't want to get in trouble and figured that, since everything was fine, it would be a one-time incident, over and never to come up again. I should have screamed really loud.

As I got older, I began to have massive panic attacks—but those were "made up," so I was "just really upset" and needed to take a nap or eat something. I remember one of my worst ones was at an ATI conference in our dorm room. These conferences only last a week, and I knew that, but I couldn't think past that moment. When I'm in one of those spirals, I can never see past the present no matter how many extravagant braiding styles I learned.

I simultaneously hated the conference and never wanted it to end. I couldn't bring my thoughts out of how full the schedule was or how I didn't like any of the food and, overall, that this was the only week I would get to see all my friends before we would once again be pen-pals, with only the possibility of seeing each other if we were able to teach at a children's seminar together. I wanted to spend every second with my friends. I wanted to make as many new friends as possible. I wanted to stay in my room and watch TV so it wouldn't hurt as much when I had to say goodbye to everyone in a few days.

I had been drilled over and over on how to respond when someone who'd just learned I was homeschooled would ask, "But what about socialization?" We had all been taught that, as the children, we needed to answer for ourselves because then people would know WE were having all our needs fulfilled and wanted for nothing. I was taught to parrot: "Oh, I don't miss out on socialization at all! You see, because my parents are taxpayers, the public school is required to allow me access to any programs I desire if my parents cannot provide an adequate equivalent, such as sports or band. My homeschooling gives me a social

ADVANTAGE, in that I am not limited to interaction with only my age group. I often socialize with the older women of the church and am able to invest far more quality time bonding with my little sister." I hated giving that answer. It was a lie every time I said it. I'm fairly certain people knew it was all a load of shit, but how do you call someone out for being suspiciously oppressive when you're making small talk while taking their order for milkshakes?

As a teenager, my only catharsis came from excoriation that was always dismissed as teenage acne. They told me my acne would be better if I stopped touching it, but I couldn't. My only relief was watching myself pick away at the imperfections within my control. My spirals of severe depression were dismissed as mood swings and my doctor tried to ease them with birth control pills. I remember being switched from pill to pill but never finding relief from the mental torment, which was eventually diagnosed as Pre-Menstrual Dysphoric Disorder (PMDD), and not merely the sinful attitude I'd inherited from Eve's punishment, and my weak attempts at rejecting the devil.

PMS is not the same as PMDD. It's ridiculous that I even feel the need to type this, but I've been told so often, "Yeah, I get super crabby too." While I appreciate the empathy, that response leans more toward dismissive than supportive. PMS versus PMDD isn't something you get to decide you have after taking a Cosmo quiz.

For decades, I've spent at least four to five days each month truly just trying to survive myself. It's like having to keep Sleeping Beauty away from spindles; if I can get past the time frame of instinctively believing I shouldn't exist, the curse is broken for another three weeks. I don't take part in any high risk activities during those days, to prevent myself from acting on a whim. Yes, I have sudden crying outbursts and get annoyed faster than I normally would, but that's in addition to my inability to shake the massive weight of feeling nearly paralyzed by the thought that the world shouldn't have me in it.

These unshakable feelings were exacerbated with motherhood and what everyone assumed was postpartum depression but a friend of mine helped me discover was actually Dysphoric Milk Ejection Reflex (D-MER), something I'd never heard of. I had spent my life looking forward to breastfeeding, but each time the twins started to eat, and each time I'd pump I instantly wanted to die. Sometimes, I would have to stop expressing milk and throw up. I could have switched to formula—and probably should have—but I didn't know expressing milk was the thing making me miserable, especially because I liked breastfeeding and liked advocating for normalizing breastfeeding in public (especially with twins). I just didn't like the feelings that came with it. As soon as I was done expressing milk, the feelings would subside. It's the same with my PMDD. If I can just survive until that moment ends, it'll all be fine.

It took years of trying to explain these issues to medical teams before finally beginning treatment. For anyone who might relate to these feelings, I've put some resources for you at the end of this chapter.

The most extreme time period of my physical and mental health came when I was 18. I had one foot in both worlds. Describing this as having felt like I was the rope in a tug of war seems too gentle. I felt as if I was being torn into pieces, each piece fully devoted to its victor. I wanted out of the world my parents had created for me, while simultaneously wanting to stay in and fully commit to the life of a pastor's wife. I knew the oppression was wrong but the simplicity of never having to be challenged academically seemed like an ideal road to take if I didn't want anyone to find out just how much I didn't know.

If I asked simple questions, people would think I was stupid; I'd spent enough of my time making sure they didn't notice I wasn't educated. I wanted to stay in the only world I had ever known. I'd spent my entire life's efforts trying to be what they wanted me to be. If I left, it would be like throwing away all I'd worked for.

At the same time, I wanted to get out and make up for all the time I'd lost. I wanted to be young while I still had time to be young. I wanted to keep working as an EMT and go on to get my paramedic license. I wanted to date. I did have a boyfriend but he was kept a secret. I wanted to date without having to sneak around, constantly worrying if I would be caught, having my brief taste of normalcy pulled from me. It was all too much and I had long forgotten how to scream really loud. I was used to secrets and having my concerns dismissed, so, instead, I internalized all of it.

As a result, I started fainting and completely blacking out if my stress level got high enough. There were days when I fainted dozens of times. I couldn't drive for a while, which meant no ambulance and no boyfriend. I did go to church a lot. I even went on a trip with the youth group out to the mega church that ran the college I planned to attend later that fall.

As I was listening to a sermon about the consequences of running away from God's will for your life, I felt I had to decide at that exact moment what choices were right for my one shot at life. I couldn't think fast enough. It was as if my mental rolodex was swirling into minute, unidentifiable shreds before my eyes. The next thing I remember is waking up and the session being over. Evidently, I had fainted, but it was dismissed as having been slain in the Spirit and my friend said no one was concerned until I began seizing. I was told repeatedly this was all conviction from above and the seizures were the devil trying to take over my mind. The exorcism they attempted to stop the seizures seems to have been ineffective. Thankfully, my parents drove 14 hours to get me and take me home. I'm so glad they took it seriously.

The blackouts and seizures continued. Eventually, the small community hospital where I'd first glimpsed teenage normalcy had me transferred and admitted to Yale for more testing. Due to my weight and only having recently turned 18, I was admitted to the pediatric floor. This caused my father to have several fights with the staff over being kept informed about all my care, due to the fact that he was "my authority." Because I was on the peds unit, it was out of the ordinary not to include parents.

At one point, he managed to steal my chart from the nurse's station. During my intake interview, he insisted on staying in the room. Once he left, I told them I'd need to repeat the interview because I couldn't give accurate answers with my father present. When he was asked to leave the room during a psychiatric consult, he firmly instructed me to give consent for him to stay. I refused and he kicked my hospital bed, which automatically got him dismissed. That was the first time I truly stood up for myself, and I did it lying in a hospital bed.

After a lifetime of internalizing the damaging messages I'd been taught, I was no stranger to hospital beds. When I was 12, I had a small bowel obstruction after it had been drilled into my head that no one would ever marry me if my poop smelled bad. ATI ran random checks at the training centers to see if it floated or not- brilliantly described by Reddit user, @thatother-hemingway after I posted a video on the topic, as "a witch trial for turds". I was over everyone's shitty judgments, so I stopped going to the bathroom. (The unmistakable smell ended up being blood from my stomach.) I'd been throwing up blood for years thanks to my ulcers. One doctor described my stomach lining and esophagus as looking like someone let a bunch of stray cats loose in there.

No longer suicidal and finally desiring to keep living, I started to see that believing everything preached to me was slowly killing me. I felt so much relief that day, talking with the hospital psychiatrist, the first adult to listen without judgement or the intent to break me. I knew I needed to go to therapy but couldn't, because therapy was where they fill your head with lies from the devil. Not only was I still on my parents' insurance, my father worked for their claims department, so he would be able to access my file at any point, even if I intercepted any mail. I hid the card with the therapist's number they gave me, in case I was able to find a way to get treatment.

My diagnosis at discharge was "Vasovagal Syncope with Idiopathic Seizures." I was set up with a neurologist and strongly advised to follow up with a mental health professional, since this was most likely a result of stress. So, what caused such extreme physical manifestations if it wasn't demons that needed to be exorcised out of me, you ask? Well, the vagus nerve is the main controller of the parasympathetic, or "fight-or-flight response." This response can be triggered by the body's extreme reaction to stress or sudden emotion. This is what is depicted when you see someone in a movie faint after hearing shocking news or seeing something overwhelming. It's why people faint at the sight of blood. When the parasympathetic nervous system is triggered, the heart rate and blood pressure drop suddenly, causing fainting or "syncope." If the syncope lasts long enough, it can result in seizure-like activity, which neurologically differs from but physically mimics epilepsy. I don't experience an "aura," as many people with epileptic seizures do. When it happens to me, it feels like a switch in my brain just shuts off. I don't know where I go, but I go somewhere my brain has created as a sudden escape when my feet can't get me out of there. It's exactly the same thing that happened to me so often as a toddler, except this time no one was yelling for me to scream really loud.

Eventually, I learned to identify triggers that would cause me to faint and tried to avoid them, but I hadn't gone to therapy. Even though I was out of the cult, the belief that depression was a choice was still deeply rooted in my mind. I was convinced I would just get over it one day. I knew it was always worse right before and during the first few days of my period because the combination of my PMDD and the excessive blood loss, only quelled by an IUD, were enough to cause me to faint on the way to the bathroom, hitting the corner of the wall so hard that I lost the ability to write certain letters for a little while.

I hated everything. I hated that this kept happening and it only made my untreated depression worse. I never wasn't depressed; I only traveled back and forth through the vast divide between the depression in which I was dying to have my life back and the depression in which I was only living until I could die. When I want to stop being a person, there is truly nothing else that matters. Sure, there are a bunch of people who would miss me. Maybe I even make life better for some people sometimes. But none of that matters and I stop seeing the point of anything. Have I done enough good that people will remember the good things and be inspired to do more, so I can go before I make any more mistakes?

The height of my depression came during what should have been the happiest time in my life, when I was engaged and first married to My Teenage Crush. I didn't tell him how bad things had gotten because he had enough of his own stress going on. One night when he was at work, I just couldn't see past that night. I attempted to overdose on over-the-counter meds.

I'd seen enough suicides at that point to know it was probably the tidiest route. He had guns, but I thought it would be extremely rude to use something he had gotten as a gift for something that would be, at the very least, a lot to clean up. I was still terrified of drowning, and he and I had both been to enough hangings to know it is one of the most eerie suicides to encounter, even for a stranger. I didn't want to do that to him. Of all the scenes I'd experienced, overdose seemed like the most peaceful.

I didn't leave a note. If they were really curious, I had enough diaries for people to read. I just went to sleep. The next morning, he came home and woke me as he got into bed. I was surprised—not that he was home, but that I woke up. I ended up telling him why I was so surprised to be awake. He said there were enough psychs to deal with at work, and told me not to make him deal with the same dumb shit at home. Then he went to sleep. I knew that if my story was going to have a hero, it wasn't going to be played by him.

I didn't intend to tell anyone else about that night, but I'd also never lost so horribly at beer pong than I did the following Cinco De Mayo. The day started out pretty great, as I met a team of friends, that included Dreamy Eyes and the Ann to my Leslie, Michelle Foley, who had agreed to join me at the March of Dimes. After the march, we all went back to my place for drinks and, eventually, the party migrated to our friends' house around the corner.

I was fairly emotional after the march because I did it in honor of the babies I'd lost. I had a steady stream of drinks going to keep myself in party mode but eventually I couldn't handle pretending to be fun anymore and wandered off to hide behind a shed. I was back there long enough for it to get dark and to become a sobbing mess. Dreamy Eyes eventually found me (I think he and Michelle were the only ones looking for me) and was not prepared for the amount of friend responsibility he was about to take on.

It was the first time we'd ever hung out with Michelle and I assumed, after that, it would be the last. Never in a million years would I have thought sitting there that night that, a few years later, I'd be writing this as Dreamy Eyes is outside grilling dinner for our parents and our twins and that Michelle would be my best friend in the entire world.

They took turns holding me as I sobbed, and for the first time in my life, someone validated how severe my depression was without once mentioning the devil. They saved my life that night. They sat and listened for what I assume was hours, as I told them I had no idea how to exist in a world where I wasn't under male authority anymore, that my new extended family hated me, and how I didn't think I'd be able to exist for the rest of my life haunted by recurring nightmares that grew more severe with each miscarriage. I didn't even know how to keep existing on the ground behind a shed between people who weren't trying to silence me for their own convenience. After I'd cried myself into exhaustion, they found my then-husband so he could take me home. A few months later, after my Unicorn Princess divorce party, they made sure I got the help I'd so desperately needed for over 20 years. I'd finally remembered to scream really loud, but had no idea what to do when someone listened.

I know this chapter is a lot to take in. It's a lot to write, too. Telling you about losing my loophole virginity felt much less vulnerable than telling you all of this. I really want to give you a happy ending before we head into what I hope are more empowering chapters, but I don't have one. I've been trying to figure out how to write one for days. I can't. Therapy and many medication adjustments have helped a lot, but this is an ongoing battle I've yet to win. Maybe not having an ending is the best I can give you right now. It means my story isn't over yet.

I cannot tell you how to heal when I am still in the midst of my own healing, but I can provide some guidance on where to find people who are experts in screaming really loud.

For thoughts of self-harm:
suicidepreventionlifeline.org or 1-800-273-8255

For domestic violence, adult abuse reports, and safe homes:
thehotline.org or 1-800-799-SAFE (7233)

For child abuse/ neglect reports:
www.childwelfare.gov or 1-800-394-3366

PMDD resources:
www.womenshealth.gov/menstrual-cycle/premenstrual-syndrome
/premenstrual-dysphoric-disorder-pmdd or 1-800-994-9662

D-MER resources:
D-mer.org

10

The Adulterous Harlot

"God created the man first and gave him tasks to perform; then God created the woman: '...I will make for him an help meet for him.' ...If Eve was created 'to aid' Adam, it is logically assumed that Adam was to have had the leadership position. He had to provide direction, or his wife would not have known how to aide or assist him... The Fall marked the beginning of the conflict over the headship of the family. No longer does the husband rule easily. He must work to retain his headship."

—Men's Manual vol. 1

According to ATI, if you are married, you're married "'til death do you part," and they take that very seriously.

I'd learned from The Basic Seminar that the world's way of preparing for marriage was the reason there is so much illness around us; it's our punishment for adultery. I'd thought that "adultery" was when one spouse cheated on the other. Turns out that's just what The World had been telling me, when actually, as Bill Gothard informed us on Basic Seminar Day 5, far more of us are guilty of adultery than we thought!

He told a story of a couple he had counseled who were on the brink of divorce. He asked if they had "known" each other prior to the wedding, using the King James definition for "know."

He was asking if they had engaged in premarital sex. When the couple admitted they had, Bill immediately informed them they could not get a divorce, since they had already committed adultery before they were even married.

Hearing that at 13 was enough to scare me into signed pledges of abstinence and a feeling of deep guilt about any twinge of attraction I may have felt. This didn't keep me from my musically-themed romantic fantasies; it just meant I felt guilty about them.

In ATI, divorce is almost as bad as homosexuality. They say that all sin is equal in the Bible, but "abomination" sounds far harsher than "adulterer." ATI blames premarital sex for every disease out there, from cancer to asthma. (Bill even released a told-you-so statement on the coronavirus.)

So, when I was 24, I did the only thing any girl in ATI was allowed to fantasize about - I got married.

I've heard that one third of all marriages end in divorce. My ex-husband and I met two other couples on our honeymoon, both of whom are still married. Their Instagrams are adorable, so I guess we proved the statistic true.

I've also heard that good marriages don't end in divorce, and I fully agree with that. This chapter is about the direction my path led me when I was fresh out of the cult. It surprised me to find so many fellow Exers are very happily divorced. I think for us it holds a level of powerful symbolism of unspeakable joy I once only thought was possible to experience during a rhema inducing altar call. I'd feel comfortable assuming the divorce rates among Exers are higher than those of The World. It's almost the norm among us. When people from The World find out I'm divorced they seem surprised. When Exers find out it almost feels as if it were expected.

Don't be angry for me. Don't write to me and tell me how young and stupid you think we were. Some probably remember the story differently, but that's how it goes with most stories. I can't write an impartial version; I can only write mine. I don't tell this story out of bitterness, nor hurt. I tell it because it was a crucial turning point in my story.

When I was 17, I met My Teenage Crush. We both worked in the same department at the local hospital. We shared our first bonding experience as a body bag ripped open on our way to the morgue. We got all the parts put back neatly, though it did take a few tries to figure out how to tuck the arms back in. Stuffing a body into a morgue fridge didn't feel like an appropriate time to bring up the fact that we each thought the other was cute.

Through the years, we each dated other people but always hung out in the same circle. We went on group vacations together and stayed up all night running 911 calls. At various times, when someone would be banned from the friend group (yep, that was a thing that took place regularly and, being freshly shunned from my original cohorts, I found it completely normal), he and I always refused to stop talking to each other. We gave each other relationship advice constantly; I guess neither of us were very good at that.

I thought we would always be friends. The first time I ever thought otherwise was the day he doubted me as a person. It stings to hear doubt from an enemy, but to hear it from the person you trust most gives you the choice to stay safe and keep trusting them or risk everything you've known in order to trust yourself.

He worked for the EMS company in the city where I had dreamed of working. After a grueling amount of competing company politics, I was hired. Ironically, it was the same day Dreamy Eyes was hired there, as well. He was hired to do the exact same job for which I had six years experience and fought for a year to get, while he had never worked on an ambulance and got the job without having met anyone. Isn't being a handsome, tall, White male great?

I couldn't wait to tell My Teenage Crush that I finally had gotten the job. When I told him, he laughed. He said I'd never make it. I'd never be able to handle "the city." I wanted that job too badly not to make it.

The first day I was "cleared" to work as a medic on my own, I had one of the worst PCP patients I've experienced. The patient slammed my partner against the inside of the ambulance, injuring his neck, and pinned me to the ceiling. We called over the radio for the police. My Teenage Crush was also working, so he and his partner came to help us before the police could get there. He held the patient while I quickly gave the medicine to calm him enough for us to care for him safely. He told me, "You'd better not miss and stab my leg." After the call was over and I was cleaning the ambulance, he said, "Hey, you didn't cry. High five!" and that night, he bought me my first Guinness.

I've always thought of that day as one of my defining moments, when I knew I was going to make it. But I was still trapped in the mindset of needing to prove myself to someone else before I could see my own worth, no matter what anyone thought about "Homeschool Heather." Spoiler: I've been at that job for 12 years.

Not long after that call, when we were both fresh out of serious breakups, he let me in on the secret that he'd had a crush on me since we met, but he said that I was too sheltered to pursue at first. We both ended up dating other people and were never single at the same time, anyway. I should have known better. For the first time in my life, though, I was finally starting to take control of my future and didn't need a relationship at the moment. I had just taken back my grandmother's diamond from a guy I dated for four years, after spending three-and-a-half years trying to muster up the courage to break up with him. I finally had the job I had worked so hard to get. I finally stopped being in committed relationships with abusive guys. My plan had been to get my own place, preferably in a city, and embrace my "prime years," the years I felt I had pried from the grasp of the cult just before it was too late.

But I was 22 and caught up in the moment of everything I had wanted at 17 actually happening. I let myself get lost in his words. I was so lost in his words that I became deaf to reason. We were an unlikely couple who made sense only to us. You know those couples who just fit? The ones who might as well be Tom Hanks and Meg Ryan? That's how we saw ourselves when, really, we were the plot point couple in the beginning of a rom-com who are destined to fail so that the protagonist can find true love.

We became so caught up in finally being able to date each other that we didn't realize when there was too much of a good thing. We picked out our kids' names on our first date (we both have kids now and did not use those names). That was in November. On New Year's Eve, he said we should get engaged. It was more of a conversation than a proposal. I thought he was kidding or at least that he meant to say he was dating me with the intention of proposing in the not-so-distant future. Nope. He told me he was serious.

I thought that this must be the way my fairytale would play out. It's a small dream, but I'd really like an actual on-one-knee-mushy-af proposal before I die. I'm 0-for-2, so my record isn't looking great. Our engagement was tumultuous and, despite discussions of calling it off, he assured me that being together was worth whatever pain presented itself.

The year we were engaged was quite possibly the most mentally disturbing year of my life. It probably was for him, as well; but this isn't his book, and I didn't ask. Planning a wedding is usually stressful, but I hear that it should also be grounded in the joy of knowing that when it's all over, you'll just be together. I wish I had felt the joy. I waited for the joy to come. Unless I was at work, I spent as much time as I could asleep. Eventually, sleep was no longer an escape and the nightmares started, so I started taking Benadryl in order to fall asleep with fewer dreams. I was excited about my dress. I was excited about our honeymoon, which would be the first time I ever left the country, outside of driving through Canada. I had the perfect invitations, venue, bridal party, even officiant. But I wasn't excited. Actually, I was suicidal.

I didn't tell him how serious my depression was because I thought he might assume that I didn't love him. I did. I didn't want him to have to worry about me in addition to the rest of the stress he had at the time.

To look back on everything, it seems blindingly obvious that we weren't meant to be. I've typed and deleted "I wish I knew then what a mistake we were making" several times; but, the thing is, I don't regret it. It was hard. It was painful. It was young and stupid and taught me more about life than I would have learned from my best friend going through it, or waiting to see if Ross and Rachel really were on a break. I needed to feel what it was like to be loved and I needed to feel the pain of having my world fall apart around me. The only thing I regret is the tertiary pain we caused our families.

I poured all of my efforts into planning the perfect wedding, subconsciously making up for all the hell that surrounded us. We made sure to choose our officiant carefully. Well, I did. He didn't really care who it was. I wanted someone we knew but hadn't been a part of my spiritual pain. The man we chose had been my "Bus Captain" through my teen years and was one of the few who didn't change his attitude towards me when I decided to drop my enrollment to his alma mater to pursue paramedicine. He may have been disappointed but, unlike the rest of the Bible-thumping critics seeking me out to yell at me for rejecting God, he told me he believed God had a plan for me to be used as a paramedic. (We've already established my love of male approval, so you know that was big for me.)

He was one of the men in my life who allowed me to understand the various levels of the Greek context of love that I had spent so many years studying. I had the same guiding role from a Sunday School teacher at our first church, as well. Those relationships allowed me to experience a love that was made of nothing but caring for my long-term wellbeing, while allowing me to make the short-term choices they knew would need to hurt in order to shape me.

Our wedding day came, bringing along the welcomed "normal" stress of a wedding. Our caterer called that morning to say they couldn't accept our credit card because we hadn't had the account for long enough. So, while I was getting my hair and makeup done, he and his groomsmen showed up at the bank in tuxes to get a bank check so our 100+ guests could eat. I didn't eat. I hear that many brides don't, though - normalcy checkmark?

The ceremony was a blur. I remember just wanting it to be over. Our parents didn't talk to each other. Someone came to get me out of the receiving line at one point because everyone thought Gramma was having a stroke. Turns out Gramma was just cold and cured with a sweater, but everyone had jumped right to stroke.

We awkwardly danced our first dance and I'm pretty sure that was the last time we saw each other until everything was over. I spent the night on the dance floor and I have no idea where he was. Looking back, it's incredibly clear that neither of us knew how to express our expectations. I went along, assuming we would be all over each other, overjoyed to be married. He didn't have the same assumption. We became so focused on fighting with the world in order to be together that we never fought for ourselves.

Once in a while, on special occasions or at his family's cabin, he would have a cigar and I would share a bit of it. We had brought a cigar with us to share that night. I thought about that moment of calm all day. After the wedding was over, we went out with a few of our friends. As I was scarfing down the most delicious poutine I'd ever tasted, I suddenly realized that My Teenage Crush had been missing from the table for quite some time. One of our friends casually told me that he was outside with a few people, having his cigar.

That shouldn't have hurt me as much as it did. Even now, every time I edit this, I feel a knot in my stomach when I get to this part. But in that moment, I felt the terrifying feeling of "What if I made a mistake?" Why would he hurt me by going to do something on his own rather than talk about a change of plans? He probably didn't even know that something so small meant so much to me, but that moment foreshadowed our undoing. I always felt like I made my desires known but sometimes it feels like I can scream out what I need and it falls on deaf ears. It's ironic; my editor pointed out that I wrote that last sentence as present tense, not past. I almost changed it, but didn't because although situations change, the frustrations I feel when I don't feel heard remain.

When he came back inside, someone informed the band that it was our wedding day and they called us up to dance. It won't surprise you to read that I loved every bit of that moment. After all, the romantic proposal of my dreams involves a flash-mob (yes, that's a not-so-subtle hint). But he is an introvert and never enjoyed the spotlight. He danced anyway, for which I am grateful.

Although I don't read too much into signs, I've always felt like the music around me has played for a reason, like a soundtrack happening just for me. Even as I type this at my favorite spot on Old Orchard Beach's pier, the band is playing "Breakfast At

Tiffany's"- a song he would play on his guitar while I'd wonder if one day we'd look at each other knowing that's the one thing we've got. Perhaps it's conceited, but there is nothing stopping anyone else from believing the world is playing their personal soundtrack, as well; in fact, I highly recommend it. As we stepped out to dance, the band began to play the song that my previous long-term boyfriend had deemed "ours." My Teenage Crush knew it. I'm pretty sure most of our friends knew it, too, since many were mutual.

We went back to the hotel that night and I gave him his wedding gift - three journals filled with letters I'd faithfully written to him every day for the year leading up to our wedding. He didn't open them. As far as I know, he's never opened them. It may have been that the day had been long enough and he was innocently exhausted but, nevertheless, he set them aside, went to bed, and I cried myself to sleep.

We went on a tropical honeymoon and then spent the first year of marriage working crazy hours and spending more time together with friends than together alone. We never fought; that should have been a warning for me, but I wanted so badly for life to work out well for us. As the months went on, he started sleeping more and more, and I spun deeper into my depression. I tried every band-aid solution I could find to make him happy but nothing seemed to work. His whole life had changed when he married me and I wanted to make him feel as comfortable as possible. When a close friend of ours suddenly passed away, I adopted one of his dogs, hoping it would help us feel more like a family. I ended up falling in love with my dog, but she only added more stress for him. He lost sleep over the barking; having to adjust to a new house all of a sudden isn't easy for a dog either.

The instinctive pit in my stomach that comes when everything seems fine but you just know things are about to change forever didn't show up until we went to breakfast with his co-worker and the co-worker offered him a dip pouch (it's basically fake chewing tobacco). I instantly laughed because someone he worked with every night should know he didn't chew. And then it hit me. I was the one who didn't know. It seems like it shouldn't be a big deal. He had a gross vice, but so what? The pit came because he had insisted on countless occasions that he didn't use dip pouches although most of his co-workers did. He lied. For as long as I'd known him and as hard as he fought for us, I had never known him to lie. Not to anyone. But he lied to me.

In the months that followed, we built the life that finally seemed to be on the path we had wanted. We bought a house that was absolutely perfect for us. The inside was cozy yet open and the outside had a patio with a bar and a yard that was screaming for a pool. We packed up my house where we had lived and picked out rugs, furniture, and paint colors for our new beginning.

On our first anniversary, we dug our wedding cake topper out of the freezer, and we gagged. Year-old cake is terrible. Why do we waste that freezer space on such a tradition?

One weekend, we went out to dinner at my then-favorite restaurant. We had everything we had ever wanted to try from the menu. We talked about our kids by name, coming home to our new house and the house warming we would host. The evening was perfect.

Then, on the two-mile drive home, everything changed. He told me to stop talking about the house and that he needed to talk to me about something. By the time we got to the driveway, he'd told me he was leaving. We went inside, sat on the couch and I asked him if he loved me anymore. I watched his eyes fill with tears and pain, as he knew he was about to break my heart with a single word.

"I don't know."

So, he did it in three words but, as I heard them, I wished there had only been one. Hearing "no" would have been an earth-shattering answer, but "I don't know" meant I could still have a chance at fixing whatever was happening, leaving me grasping at any sliver of hope I could find.

He packed some clothes and his guitar that night and left, saying he needed some time to think, and I didn't hear from him for two weeks. If you've ever been through a breakup, you know how confusing it is to be the one who is left. I was understandably more upset than I knew I was capable of being. I had no idea what to do with these emotions, or the house, or the dog, or anything my future was supposed to be.

I knew I was upset to the point at which I was no longer safe, so I packed a suitcase and showed up at Dreamy Eyes' apartment. He was one of my closest, platonic friends and the most reasonable person I knew who would be emotionally distant enough to handle my situation. I told him I was going to sleep on his couch until I didn't feel like dying anymore and that I needed someone to help me go to work (we had the same schedule) and remind me to eat. He did. He's very good at being the person to comfort someone during their most difficult hour. I think that's what makes him a fabulous ER doctor. He's by far the person you want by your side when your world is crashing and you need to hand over all responsibility to someone else. He's able to remove all emotion and focus on the practical, which is what I needed more than anything in that moment, when emotion was all I could see.

For two weeks, I had no idea what was happening. I don't remember much more than the pain of not knowing what would happen to everything I had known to be stable in my life. I saw My Teenage Crush during those two weeks. By then, he was an ER nurse and I was a medic so we saw each other a few times every night. I also saw his coworker, who would soon be his new wife; everyone knew it as well as I did. I had said dozens of times that I hadn't thought their level of friendship was appropriate, that it made me uncomfortable, but - tale as old as time - I was the wife paranoid of "nothing."

I had two houses hanging in the balance, and I didn't want to go through with a sale on the one I owned alone, in case I needed to keep it. I found out I was pregnant but I didn't tell him. I didn't want him to come back just because he was stuck.

It didn't matter anyway because I lost the baby a week later. I'd miscarried before, so I knew that familiar tearing pain of feeling a life detach itself from your body. I know that child would not have had an easy family life, by any means, but it doesn't take away the heartbreak in the moment. It doesn't make passing the clots of blood that had started to grow into my child any easier, but it helped me want to push away the husband who had helped create that pain.

Having to break the news to my family that I was getting divorced was far more difficult than when I had taken my father out in public to tell him I was engaged to a man who hadn't asked permission to marry me. You know that quote from Billy Graham's wife, "I don't believe in divorce, but I belive in murder"? I'm surprised none of my relatives have that cross-stitched on throw pillows. Throughout my whole family tree, we have rapists, incestual pedophiles, child molesters, spouse and child abusers, thieves, drug addicts, and a murderer. But I was the first one ever to get a divorce. My family simply didn't believe in divorce because, you know, it's important to have standards.

I became "Poor Cousin Heather" to my extended family, even after months of assuring everyone I was very sorry for their having wasted money on wedding gifts but also very, very at peace with where I was in life. My mother was sad, which is reasonable; divorce is really fucking hard. My father seemed disappointed in me because it was happening but also because I didn't fight it. I willingly went with My Teenage Crush on the day he filled the papers, so I could be served right then and set a court date. Why prolong the inevitable? I didn't want to be with someone who didn't want to be with me. I didn't hate him, so it made no sense for us to make each other miserable when all we needed to do was walk away.

My father asked me how I would handle the idea of being single for the rest of my life, seeing as how a "good Christian man" wouldn't marry me now that I was an adulterous harlot. This wasn't just my father's opinion. It didn't matter that I'd forsaken all others during my marriage or that he was the one leaving. All that mattered was that in the end, I'd be divorced, which Biblically equaled adultery. Even though I couldn't make him stay if I'd wanted to, "good Christian men" would always see me as an adulteress, since I had vowed "'Til death do us part" and I would not be able to marry in good conscience unless My Teenage Crush died. None of this was news to me. I grew up knowing a handful of single parents who had been divorced but refused to remarry or even date because, in God's eyes, they were still bound to their living ex.

I didn't go to my parents' church anymore but I kept in contact with some of the people there who hadn't hurt me. "S" was one of them and he was one of the few who called to see how I was doing. S' wife had divorced him a few years before and he was amongst those I knew who stayed single to avoid further adultery. He listened without judgement and warned me that the first few months would be extremely difficult, that I would need to guard my heart more than ever since now I'd been "sexually awakened." But this was the first time in my adult life that I was actually single for more than five minutes. I'd spent my entire life either in a cult, safety pinning my shirt gaps closed, or married. If I'd need to worry about guarding any of my parts, my heart definitely wasn't at the top of that list.

For the first time in my life, I felt powerful. I learned to mow my own lawn and fix my own house. I learned that I love the adventures I can have when I'm on my own. It had never been a fight, but I love to talk to every stranger around me, and this would often embarrass him, so I had toned it down. After he served me the papers, I went alone to my favorite place on earth, New York City. I got myself a fancy hotel room and had dinner at the Waldorf. No longer toning down my social interactions, I met a woman who was also dining alone because her husband was on a business trip. We ended up having dinner together and then walking around the city until our feet hurt and I needed to buy flats.

I've worn those flats almost every warm day because they remind me of the first time I knew I'd make it on my own. It was in my hotel room, sitting in the white accent chair in the corner, that I decided to write a book. This book.

In order to accept the reality of becoming a Ms., I'd either need to live with the guilt-ridden title of "Adulterous Harlot" or reject everything I'd been taught to believe about relationships. I didn't want to go out and find a new husband to take care of me. I wanted to enjoy the sudden second chance to be whoever I wanted. I had to decide which baggage I was going to pack and carry forward and which to leave behind. I was terrified that I'd be instantly dismissed as an eventual wife if I was divorced at 25, but I slowly learned that anyone who cared wasn't someone who I wanted in my life.

The day finally came when we had to go to divorce court. I went to the mall to get my hair and makeup done because I tend to cry less if I'm invested in how my mascara looks. The women who created my look were fully dedicated to making me as fabulous as possible, putting in all the energy they had from men who had hurt them. It was a morning of catty wonderfulness.

We walked into court together and found our places between all the other ghosts of couples past. We sat in the courtroom waiting for our turn, which came last because of our "W" last name. As we watched marriages end before our eyes, we exchanged hand squeezes and handkerchiefs, grateful we hadn't walked in with the intention of ruining the other's lives. The judge noted I was waiving my request for alimony and asked if I was aware this was my only chance to collect the money that would afford me the life to which I had been accustomed. I knew, and I made enough of my own money to live quite happily. We were granted our divorce and my last name was legally moved back to the H's.

After court, we went out for drinks, feeling the peace that comes when something is finally right, even though there is immense pain. I gave him back his handkerchief and we held each other, not because we were in love anymore but because there was no one else on the planet who knew what that specific hurt felt like.

My best friends were waiting for me that afternoon with a cake that said "Happy Unicorn Princess Day!" If I was going to change my title from "wife," it wouldn't be changing to "Adulterous Harlot," and they decided on "Unicorn Princess." We watched movies, ordered all the junk food within miles, drank all the wine there was, and I started to write.

11

Goddesses Aren't
Blasphemous

"Many daughters have done virtuously, but thou excellest them all."

—Proverbs 31:29

That was the main theme for ATI's "Excel." Excel was similar to CharacterFirst!, in that it had its own training center and young adult females would head there to complete an eight-week training program. I only ever attended Pre-Excel, which was the kids' version, much like the Children's Institute is a miniature Basic Seminar.

Prior to attending the weeklong sessions during our first trip to Knoxville, I was required to memorize Proverbs 31:10-31, which is the passage about "The Virtuous Woman." As you may have guessed, there was a song that went along with it. My mother loved this passage long before ATI was a factor and had memorized it when I was very young. To help her remember, she illustrated posters of Cinderella performing all her chores and matched each verse to an action. These posters adorned our hallway for years; they are probably the reason I still remember almost a full chapter of the Bible and why I was able to memorize it at 9 years old. (See, this book isn't just about me complaining that my mother screwed me up.)

In case you haven't read it, here's the King James version I memorized:

Proverbs 31:10 Who can find a virtuous woman? for her price is far above rubies.

11 The heart of her husband doth safely trust in her, so that he shall have no need of spoil.

12 She will do him good and not evil all the days of her life.

13 She seeketh wool, and flax, and worketh willingly with her hands.

14 She is like the merchants' ships; she bringeth her food from afar.

15 She riseth also while it is yet night, and giveth meat to her household, and a portion to her maidens.

16 She considereth a field, and buyeth it: with the fruit of her hands she planteth a vineyard.

17 She girdeth her loins with strength, and strengtheneth her arms.

18 She perceiveth that her merchandise is good: her candle goeth not out by night.

19 She layeth her hands to the spindle, and her hands hold the distaff.

20 She stretcheth out her hand to the poor; yea, she reacheth forth her hands to the needy.

21 She is not afraid of the snow for her household: for all her household are clothed with scarlet.

22 She maketh herself coverings of tapestry; her clothing is silk and purple.

23 Her husband is known in the gates, when he sitteth among the elders of the land.

24 She maketh fine linen, and selleth it; and delivereth girdles unto the merchant.

25 Strength and honour are her clothing; and she shall rejoice in time to come.

26 She openeth her mouth with wisdom; and in her tongue is the law of kindness.

27 She looketh well to the ways of her household, and eateth not the bread of idleness.

28 Her children arise up, and call her blessed; her husband also, and he praiseth her.

29 Many daughters have done virtuously, but thou excellest them all.

30 Favour is deceitful, and beauty is vain: but a woman that feareth the Lord, she shall be praised.

31 Give her of the fruit of her hands; and let her own works praise her in the gates.

One of the illustrations my mom drew was Cinderella sitting on a scale, comparing her worth to rubies and far outweighing them. This is the reason I picked a faux ruby in my second wedding ring rather than a diamond (That's really more on the prideful side than it is romantic, seeing as I picked it out and bought it myself because I knew no man could pick out exactly what I wanted, let alone fully appreciate my worth).

I have lived and breathed Proverbs 31 for so long that I thought I knew all there was to know. For a woman in a cult, that chapter is your only job description. I always thought verse 29 meant that if we all just stayed in our place and did what was expected of us, God would end up rewarding, or excelling us all. It wasn't until I was rereading it to make sure my punctuation was correct for this book that I discovered the T in "Thou" is lowercase, changing the entire direction of this chapter. (And here I thought I had outgrown my rhema phase.) Little did I know, I'd stumble upon a plethora of deconstructing rhemas as this chapter unfolded. This is the chapter I've taken out and put back several times because it reads more like my diary than a book I wrote for you. I finally decided to keep it in because much like my diaries full of thinking errors and words needing to be changed to call out evil for what it is, it depicts where I am in my journey of deconstructing in real time.

All this time, I'd thought God just pushed all the girls through inspection because it didn't really matter if you contributed to the world or not, as long as you could be a wife. I feel I have valid cause to have arrived at that conclusion, seeing as all I'd ever been told was to be like all the other girls and do as I'm told by my father or husband.

But that isn't what it means! That lowercase "thou" means the virtuous woman surpassed everyone else; she pushed harder and made a difference to those around her. Reading that passage now doesn't make me feel like the virtuous woman was some uneducated, husband-pleasing sub, as she had been painted by ATI. She seems like a lady who gets shit done. Yes, she has a husband but, to me, it reads more like he's doing his thing as she's busy being virtuous AF.

During my sister's homeschool graduation party, I watched as she opened gifts from other members of her church (I had already left at this point). She received a lot of books on how to be a wife, mother, and cook, but nothing in regards to further education. I wanted to mention it but my mother told me I had to shut up and not ruin the party.

One woman there caught my attention; she wanted to ask me a few questions about homeschooling, since she had only ever spoken with homeschooling parents and never an adult homeschool alumni. Not only did she want to homeschool—she was champing at the bit to be a fully submissive ATI family.

This was back in my very early overcoming days, when feminism was terrifying and not many people knew the extent to which I was putting together the puzzle pieces of patriarchy.

The woman asked me to tell her about all the advantages I had in life thanks to ATI's methods. My mother overheard and mentioned that asking me wasn't a great idea, but she was too late. I can be diplomatic when I want to, so, in an extremely generous effort not to cause a scene, I simply told her I'd been trying to get into college, but doing so without adequate transcripts or courses meant I had to go through dozens of extra hoops and basically convince the entire admissions board I could handle their classes, despite having nothing to put in front of them to back up my confidence. Trying to get into medic school and college was a lot like the pig in the book "Rufus Goes To School," when the pig has all the desire in the world to learn even though the principal keeps telling him he can't come to school. In the end, Rufus doesn't take that shit and keeps trying until they believe he can learn.

I told the woman if she insisted on homeschooling, she should, by all means, go with a different curriculum so her kids wouldn't have to fight their way out of a hole simply to reach everyone else's lowest baseline for education. She laughed at me and said she wasn't worried about college readiness; she only had daughters. She later told my mother I was rude for telling her that no possible good could come from me continuing to speak to her and then walking away before she could give a response. I think that was pretty damn nice of me, seeing as it meant not ruining my sister's party by breaking into a full-on soapbox rendition of "Ya got Trouble, with a capital T, and that rhymes with C, and that stands for Cult!"

When you're a girl in a cult, no one ever asks what you want to be when you grow up. They only ask, "How many kids do you want to have?!" or "Is God calling you to marry a pastor or a missionary?!" Your destiny is all laid out for you. You get two options. My plan was to marry a missionary because it meant I'd get to take geography classes. Sometimes medical classes, too, since a lot of missionaries ran free clinics. Being a pastor's wife who polices where hemlines fall against youth group members' knees seemed like I'd hit the peak of my calling too early.

I was out of ATI because I had "graduated" and didn't want to go to their "college," so I planned to attend Hyles Anderson College in Hammond, IN, which is basically a fundie factory. You may have heard of it when their former pastor sexually assaulted a sixteen-year-old girl. Although Hyles Anderson/First Baptist Church wasn't part of ATI, it was a frying-pan-into-the-fire situation. There were nearly no requirements to be accepted, other than a calling from God, so I figured I'd take my only shot at a semi-standard life experience and apply. Even though HAC was as fundie as they get, I still had to beg my father to let me apply because my parents never intended for me to go to college. I ended up making a bold move, going out from under my umbrella of protection and talking directly with our preacher. With his help, my father agreed to let me go.

Even though I don't like teaching at all, I was going to go for early childhood education. All my life, I've been told how great I am with kids and how I was meant to be a mom. It only occurred to me as I wrote this that it was all grooming. None of those statements were based on my behaviors; it was all them trying to shape me into who they wanted me to be. I like my kids and my friends' kids, but I'm not someone who is "good with kids." I hate arts and crafts. Hate them. I don't like playing games. I don't like getting dirty. I don't like making a mess. I'm really bad at the whole giving-all-of-myself-to-another-human thing. Kids give me anxiety because, other than my own kids, I have no idea how to relate to them. What do you even say to a kid if you're not trying to get them to pray for salvation?

But, nevertheless, ATI had groomed me into thinking I was great with kids and should become a teacher. It was either that or major in "Marriage and Motherhood" and, even as a fundie, that major made me cringe.

In the months leading up to the beginning of "college," I applied to the EMS agency within walking distance of campus. When one of the advisors called to ask me if I'd applied to any of the approved jobs in the area, I told her I had. Well, apparently that wasn't true. EMS was not one of the approved jobs for women attending their school. Women were limited to telemarketing, secretarial work, and house cleaning, none of which remotely interested me. I told the advisor I had already spent a few years as an EMT, so, ideally, getting hired there shouldn't be too difficult. But, alas, this was against school policy because I would be required to wear pants. Even off campus and worn for safety and necessity, pants on women were forbidden.

I had no idea who I would be if I didn't follow the path they'd planned for me, but I knew I couldn't let the EMT—the one part of myself I'd fallen in love with—die. In what was probably the most crucial page turn in my choose-your-own-adventure story, I rescinded my acceptance and applied for paramedic school.

For weeks, I got calls from the college staff admonishing me for my choice, screaming into the phone prayers of protection from the devil, who had clearly taken over my frontal lobe. According to them, I'd rejected God's design for me as a woman by taking a masculine job. I'd cast every last pearl before swine by throwing away my chance to marry a preacher boy with standards. There was no going back.

As I navigated my way through this new world in which I could make my own choices, I would hear people talking about how great it is to be a feminist. Even though I'd left the cult, I was far from ready to accept a new label, especially one I'd only ever known as a negative. My 2004 diary is filled with reasons I hated feminists. As far as I knew, feminism meant rejecting everything about being female. Nothing would be pretty; I couldn't wear dresses or do my hair or love pink. I'd have to stop shaving my legs and hate all men. I couldn't be a Christian and a feminist—that was an impossible overlap. I'd have to be a working mom because feminists were never stay-at-home moms.

That's the thing about deconstructing: you can physically walk away from everything, but you bring along all the thinking errors because there's no way to distinguish what's true anymore. You have to relearn all of it and, as far as I know, there's no crash course on how to be a well-adjusted, functioning human. So, it's a process.

When I was little, I fantasized about having my own house and kids. Actually, I still fantasize about that as I've been interrupted multiple times when all I want to do is approve the spots where Lorna suggests I should add a comma. I loved sneaking out into the kitchen to get my mother's beautifully displayed home organization book and read all about how to multitask and clean every area of your house. Maybe that's why I love vacuuming so much.

I knew how to fold a fitted sheet long before minimalists made it cool. I didn't want to stop liking pretty things. I still want to be swept off my consensual feet (Lorna suggested I change that to past tense, but I can't since I'm still waiting). But I also want to mow the lawn, build fires, replace toilets, and lift weights. I want to cook and be cooked for. I want to be beautiful and capable. I still want to be wooed. I want giant dresses and hats but also cargo pants and a tie. No one ever told me you can have your cake and bake it too.

I'm very lucky to have been born into the body with the sex best matching my identity. I love being a girl (while I identify as a cis-female, calling myself a "woman" has never felt comfortable.

When people share my videos on social media, they'll caption them with "This woman from a cult..." and I always think they must mean someone else. It's going on the list of things to explore when I stop firing therapists for not being Paula); as much as PMDD has stolen my life, I actually like having a period. I like having the advantage of being a female when we have a patient who prefers such for their care, even if it means taking more calls than I'd need to.

Nope, there was no room for feminism in my new life until the day my friend congratulated me on becoming one and I quickly corrected her. She caught on right away that I still had a skewed definition of feminism and explained to me that, while there are extremes of any belief, the concept of feminism is merely believing men and women are equal. She changed my life that day. She showed me it was possible to believe in the foundation of beliefs without buying into extremism. It was completely freeing to discover I could be a feminist without becoming an athiest. Who knew?! I've since adopted Garfunkel and Oates' song "50/50" as my ode to feminism. If I ever recite wedding vows again, I'll be reciting that song.

When I left the cult, I was very intentional that I didn't leave God, just the people and places that hurt me. I left their extremism, not my faith. I cathartically swear, a lot, but I still won't say any "God swears," as I call them. I never want to be guilty of blasphemy (I had a REALLY hard time watching "The Book Of Mormon" for that reason) and I'd always been taught the most offensive form of blasphemy was taking the Lord's name in vain, which I was told happened when someone said, "Oh My God" (Even now, that made me nauseous to type and I will probably not say it on the audiobook).

Needless to say, this confused the fuck out of me when the apprenticeship choir was made to sing the hymn "And Can It Be." Fun fact, that's my all-time favorite hymn, but I didn't tell anyone because I figured it had slipped its way into our new hymnals and the ultra-fundies just hadn't caught it. I loved playing it on my violin so I didn't point it out to my father, who was in charge of the church's music. The third verse goes, "'Tis mercy all immense and frEEeee, but oooOOOOooo my GoooOOOOoood it fooOOOuund out me." I spent years being conflicted over this song and, moreover, wondered why ATI would ever have 2,000 of us sing it at a conference. I was convinced this was a Spiritual test and we'd all failed. It was the only explanation for being directed to sing that!

Even though I'd obeyed, sang, and fallen in love with that song, it was the ONLY time I'd ever say those words sober or not mid-orgasm and, even then, it's very rare for me not to find a less blasphemous substitute. I refused to use them casually. I don't think I'll ever get to the point of using God's name before the word "damn." Even hearing it makes me extremely uncomfortable, but I've stopped instinctively smacking people who do say it.

I was so terrified of idolatry, I wouldn't watch Hercules because I knew there were gods in it and wasn't about to go to Hell for a Disney movie. We finally watched it last week because the twins hadn't seen it and my husband thought it was hilarious to watch me glare at the TV for claiming a falsehood as "the Gospel truth". I hummed through the parts in "You're Welcome" when Maui claimed he was a demigod because I didn't want anything sounding as if I were claiming to be God to cross my lips. Yep. Moana only came out in 2016 and I physically left all forms of religious cults in 2008. This shit just keeps kicking around in my brain's Rolodex.

It wasn't until I was well into writing this book that I even learned there is more than one way to use the Lord's name in vain. I looked it up to include a small bit on swearing in this chapter, and ended up accidentally deconstructing for several hours. According to many fellow deconstructionist scholars out there, saying "Oh my god" isn't even remotely close to the blasphemy we are trying to avoid! In fact, we were all trained to do it!

I've been reading that "using God's name in vain" actually means you should not take on the title of Christian nor Believer if you are going to be a shitty person who makes people want nothing to do with your God. There are examples of evangelists promising blessings in exchange for offerings or deliberately robbing a child of their education, claiming it's "God's will." That harming people, using them for your own agenda in the name of your "ministry," or committing terrible acts, like forming a cult in God's name, is the actual crime.

Mind. Blown.

Rolodex pages everywhere.

The things I'd been trained to do, the way I'd learned to treat people—THAT was the blasphemy?! Oh. My. god. (It's lower case because I'm still coming to terms with all of this.) I dragged my sister-in-law down this rabbit hole with me because she's super smart and used to be a pastor, so I'm constantly in awe of her deconstruction wisdom. Her initial thought was both aspects, the word use and the abusive acts can be defined as taking the Lord's name in vain, with one being a much larger offense than the other. All those times I'd been locked in my room, all the oppression, the education of which I was robbed, the medical care I was refused—they did that all in God's name. God didn't hurt me; the people who took God's name in vain did.

After several hours (ok, days) of that rhema—that's right, I'm claiming this as a rhema and there's nothing you blasphemers can do about it—I dove into Greek mythology to read about gods and goddesses. You've probably gotten there on your own by now (you're so impressive!) but, if gods were bad, I was taught that goddesses were about as deep into the blasphemy pit as you could get. If a woman should never have authority over a man, there was no place in our minds for such a sinful descendant of Eve, although some suggest Lucifer's mother is a goddess.

We were frequently warned about falling prey to the temptress nature of those proclaiming to be goddesses. Although we were allowed to buy razors, we had to boycott the Venus brand for claiming goddess status in their commercials. Wisdom Booklet 17 taught us to witness to people by telling them the meaning of their name. However, if they had a name like Donna, with a negative meaning like "moon goddess," you should never use that meaning, and instead find a meaning that will turn her attention to God.

Goddesses were not only blasphemous but, as my twins say when flabbergasted, *gaps!*, they were the root of feminism, the very belief that could take down the whole cult. At one point, someone told me to act like the goddess I am and I was convinced it was an insult equivalent to the ultimate insult used to describe female anatomy.

Looking at gods and goddesses as they were meant to be presented in Greek mythology was nothing like learning about ATI's groomed Wisdom Booklet version. I loved it! First of all, it's fascinating. Second of all, mythology is in the name; I knew going in I wasn't going to take it as Gospel (no matter what those singing Muses say). But learning about their stories and how Greek mythology ties into language and traditions captivates me.

Once in a while, I'll remember a deeply rooted way of thinking and Google it to see what the world actually says, rather than what I was told the world says. Did you know that the very offensive word for female anatomy is not even a synonym for "goddess"?! Not once did I find a non-cult site defining a goddess as anything other than extremely positive. Even the dictionary defines it as "a woman who is adored, especially for her beauty." A WOMAN. Human. Not an idol. Not God. A woman. The more I read, the more familiar these definitions sounded. Wikipedia describes a goddess as a woman "linked with virtues such as beauty, love, sexuality, motherhood, creativity, and fertility." There are pages and pages of definitions like this (which is why I'm comfortable citing Wikipedia in this case) and, maybe it's just me, but I can't help thinking these all sound terribly synonymous to a virtuous woman.

Rarely does my deconstruction process go full circle like that, but it's incredibly enlightening when it does. The Proverbs 31 woman would be considered a goddess, feminists can be feminine, and forming a cult was the blasphemous act all along!!! Deconstructing can feel a lot like when the gang pulls the mask off the monster in Scooby-Doo. I thought this chapter, originally meant to be about equality, was going to be the simplest to write. Then, it took me in a direction I hadn't intended, but I am coming out the other side feeling it was exactly what I needed to read, and just hadn't been written yet.

I discovered my inner goddess in this book. She is virtuous AF. Thank you for holding my journey in your hands.

12

When The Hero Becomes The Villain

"According to God's law, protecting the child's life is one of the basic duties of an earthly father. The Bible makes no exception for sex, intellect, or for born or unborn children."

—Wisdom Booklet 32

No one joins a cult because they are out looking to be oppressed. No one willingly enters into a church, job, nor relationship with the intention of destroying their sense of self. But how often do we see it happen? I'm sure you can think of a person close to you who is in that type of situation right now; and as hard as it is to admit, maybe it's even you.

So, how does it happen time and time again? It happened to me because all I wanted was to feel like I belonged or that someone cared about me. In looking for that, I lost myself. In every situation and relationship I've ever had, I became whoever they wanted me to be, and I'm still paying the price for it.

Honestly, it's easy to be in a cult. Hollywood has made cults out to be extremely dramatic practices, requiring you to be fully devoted, sacrificial offerings, but the truth is most aren't like that.

It was much easier to be in ATI or to be an IFB because I didn't have to decide how I felt about anything. Everything was black and white, sin or not sin. There was no in-between. It was a world where everything was perfectly clear. I didn't have to fight for anything; God would handle it. I didn't have to care about human rights because everyone deserved the suffering they endured.

It's a world where cops are always right and everyone with a penis is a boy. Where scantily clad women brought rape upon themselves, and pro-life only protects those who live in a uterus, not a shelter or a cage at the border of a "free" country. Where I trusted the words a pastor had heard in a dream and denied the words of well-read scientists.

Sometimes, I miss it, the simplicity of not worrying about the world around me. Not because I knew God was in control, but because I had and used the privilege to ignore any suffering that didn't make me look good—you know, missions trips and the general "white savior" rhetoric we love to flaunt.

Before I blocked her, I saw a post from a woman on Instagram showing a city burning to the ground, labeled "The rest of the world," next to a picture of Maria Von Trapp composing "Doe A Deer," labeled "Homeschooling moms." At first, I thought it was a meme calling out the privileged blinders homeschoolers love to wear, and shouldn't have been taken aback to see it was shared as a positive of her ability to ignore suffering. She pretty much nailed the whole "ignorance is bliss" model of living.

That's not what I want my bliss to be anymore. I can't sit idly by as the world suffers around me and not at least try to do something about it. Through all of this, I have kept my belief in God and I cannot fathom God being pleased with me picking up a guitar so as to turn my back on my neighbors. I acknowledge I am still privileged, if not more so than I used to be, and able to live a comfortable life without much worry. I will never know true, unrelenting oppression based on where I was born or the color of my skin. Although I've left behind the blindfold of the cult, I am still surrounded by the ignorance of my privilege. Thanks to friends who aren't afraid to tell me when I'm being an asshole, I have been kicking against the pricks of fundamentalism and trying to open my mind to the world around me.

It's uncomfortable. Very uncomfortable.

I've drawn a great deal of my inspiration for this chapter from my twins' constant desire to watch "The Descendents" movies. Of all the Disney movies out there, I never thought that would be the one to make me feel the most seen. "When you're evil, doing less is doing more" perfectly puts into words why I regretfully stayed silent while witnessing the oppression of others. I figured doing nothing was better than actively hurting someone. I now know it's just as evil.

I was used to "worldly, humanistic" people telling me that everything ATI led me to believe was a lie, but finally hearing them and accepting it as truth is an entirely different process. It doesn't matter how many scientific facts or how many people try to rescue someone they love from the grasps of their ways; if a person isn't ready to listen, it will do no good. We just dig our heels in that much deeper.

And it's not always as profound as you'd expect. It's the little things. Recently, on social media, I read the lyrics to a children's song from a popular Christian cartoon about a cheeseburger with "#purityculture" in the caption. Well, I made the internet very angry at me. They said I was taking my deconstruction way too far and reading too much into it, trying to tear apart everything instead of sticking to the cult. Well, in the words of Ferris Buller, "You can never go too far."

I get it. I took something you loved and I showed you how it's hurting someone else. I made your hero the villain. It's much easier to insult me in 140 characters than it is to reexamine a good memory from your past. I would have reacted the same way back when I was fully immersed in cult life, but now there's a devil on my shoulder where the angels used to be.

We've all heard the stories of the serial killer whose neighbors think they're quiet and would never hurt a fly, and we think, "Yeah, but that's because they didn't really know them." But what about the people we love? What about when they're the ones silently hurting people, or even hurting us. It's so much easier and momentarily more satisfying to get angry and defend what you've always known to be your comfort zone. Learning that someone you once turned to for all the answers, all the comfort and peace you knew, is, in fact, the bad guy is devastating.

I want to acknowledge that your grief in that is real. You're not just losing the person you thought you knew; you're seeing them in a way you don't want to believe is possible. It hurts. It's so much easier to deny the abuse and keep blissfully making matching outfits out of drapes than to sneak out of a theatre full of Nazis. It's easier to stand on the outside and learn about these unfortunate, sheltered kids stuck in a cult from books that read like fiction, remaining certain that none of the gaslighting peripheries have reached you.

Trust me, I get it. I used to think this betrayal of protection would only happen in the cult (once I actually realized I was in a cult). I used to think that once I changed from someone who stood in line for hours to meet Bill Gothard to someone who never wants to see him again, it was over. Now, it feels like as long as I'm willing to trust someone, it's possible they'll disappoint me too.

When I left ATI, I was still hopelessly devoted to the IFB pastors whose approval I would have done anything in the world to win. I saw ATI as the villain, but because ATI is non-denominational, I failed to see the immense overlap in their abusive practices and poured all my energy into the church. I saw the church as a place where I could thrive but instead found myself stripped of all my beloved church roles without so much as an explanation, something no one thought was owed to a 19-year-old girl. The preacher, once my hero, shattered my little Baptist heart over and over again until I could no longer willingly be a part of a community that didn't prioritize the safety of children.

Although I am referring to ATI when I write about "the cult," many of the teachings overlap through the various churches, seminars, and leaders I've followed. Wisdom Booklet 32 teaches: "Earthly fathers are to follow the example of our Heavenly Father in the discipline of their children. Lack of correction and discipline will harm a child and will ultimately bring shame to the parents... A father also has the legal duty to control his children. The law gives him the power to establish rules of conduct and to enforce them. To accomplish this, a father may use spanking or other forms of physical restraint or punishment. A child has no right to resist moderate punishment, whether it consists of a verbal correction or physical retribution. By law the chastisement must be reasonable and moderate and done for the welfare of the child."

ATI has become extremely skilled in teaching tactics that will cause pain to a child but won't raise any flags in the systems. They encourage physical punishment, but are careful to stay on the cusp of legality, never advising breaking the law in written, nor recorded word. Note their very intentional wording: they don't advise you not to abuse your children, only to be wary of what the law allows.

In pouring through ATI's materials to write this, I nearly titled this book "Legally Abused," only deciding on "Lovingly" due to my mother's attitude going into ATI. She wasn't looking for a way to beat me and get away with it; she fell into the role of a mandatory abuser after they convinced her it was the only way to love her children.

When I read that paragraph from Wisdom Booklet 32 online, my mother replied—not in an attempt to defend herself, but to learn—asking about the parable of the good shepherd who breaks the leg of the wandering sheep, the parable most often used to justify and mandate beating the fuck out of us. The parable teaches us that if a sheep is prone to wander and endanger itself, the shepherd will break the sheep's leg but then carry the injured sheep on his shoulders until the sheep is healed. This is said to cause the sheep to become endeared to the shepherd and learn that while going astray will lead to pain, obedience will be rewarded with love. I was very familiar with the parable but hadn't thought about it as one of the concepts of gaslighting, mostly because there are just so many that it's nearly impossible to remember every one of them, especially when they are just a normal part of the narrative that shaped you.

So, I looked it up. The Bible says, "Thy rod and thy staff, they comfort me," yet we hear from the pulpit that the rod is also used to break the wandering sheep's leg. Being carried by the shepherd while the leg heals is said to endear the sheep to the shepherd and the shepherd to that sheep, the Nightingale effect, if you will.

As I have learned by actually looking into the traditions myself, many of the Jewish teachings stolen by Christians have become incredibly flawed. This is one of the many reasons I identify as a Believer and not a Christian, since Christians are what truly ruined Christianity for me. But I digress.

I've read that, in reality, breaking a sheep's leg and carrying around those 75 pounds can severely limit the care the shepherd is able to give to the rest of the flock. Additionally, the leg may never heal properly, causing the sheep to become permanently disabled and susceptible to predators. Also, the sheep may associate the rod with harm rather than protection, making the shepherd's job much more difficult. In summary, it was all a fucking lie so they could convince us that abuse was love.

I thought once I walked away from the abuse I'd finally identified it would be over. I knew the world could be a cruel place, but I expected it to be a lot more people trying to convince me to smoke cigarettes and try gay stuff than it turned out to be. No one has even offered me a cigarette, let alone tried to peer pressure me into smoking one.

I left the cult for the solace of EMS, I had no idea what was normal for "The World" and what was evil in a different body. I was touched against my will more times than I remember. I was woken up with a non-consensual kiss without so much as a "prick your finger or have an apple" before curling up on the ambulance bench. For all I knew, that's what The World was like and the reason ATI forbade Disney movies. So, I resigned myself to the fact that this was my new life. It wasn't until years later that I learned it was rude to have been habitually woken up by having balls slapped in my face by whoever wanted to sit on the couch I was on. It didn't hurt, it was just annoying; so, I didn't say anything and started sleeping on the top bunk because it's a lot harder to get teabagged at that angle. #solutions, right?

By the time I went to medic school, I was fairly used to the way the guys in EMS acted and I just accepted it. I truly believe my teacher cared about us. He is the one who saw potential in me and didn't kick me out when I'd write Biblical answers on my tests. Instead, he met me where I was and taught me in a way I was able to understand. He was very strict about us getting our assignments done on time and never missing a clinical rotation, but made light of it by having those who were late or missed an assignment "paddled" by one of my female classmates who was assigned paddling duty. I thought everyone seemed awkward about it because we were adults and too old for spankings; I had no idea there was any type of kink associated with it.

I did run late a few times, but I refused to be paddled. It was the first time I stood up for myself in the real world, and it wasn't even for the reason most would refuse. I was just completely over being hit. I told my teacher that, even though it was a joke to them, I was having no part of it; my refusal was out of pure cult exhaustion. I didn't leave a cult to get hit somewhere else. There wasn't really anything he could do about it. He didn't know I never thought to report it, so I was left alone. The rumor was that it didn't matter if I was paddled or not; girls didn't really have a place in that kink anyway. My refusal was no one's loss.

As time went on, the rumors of what was happening with the guys grew more intense but, as with most vile topics in EMS coping strategies, it was always turned into a joke. I'm ashamed I took part in laughing about it. I never thought anything of the rumors, especially because I really thought that was all they were. I had no idea anyone was actually coming to any harm. We all knew he was a strange dude, but most of us could attribute our nine-lettered shoulder patches to him, and we were grateful.

Then, one day, the rumor switched from joke to accusation. One person came forward and reported their story that we all, at least I, thought was a rumor. For the sake of legality, I cannot say whether he was guilty or not, since there was never a trial and I wasn't a victim. Not long after the accusation, the teacher many of us loved took his own life. A few dozen of us met up later that week to hold an unofficial debriefing/memorial/emergency deconstruction session together. For me, the feeling of my hero being someone's villain was all too familiar. I watched as my friends tried to work through this feeling for the first time. I locked eyes with those who had been to this rodeo before. We held each other as we were unsure whether to grieve for our loss or hide our sadness out of our true support for those who came forward.

From the outside, it's easy to say there is no room to grieve such a loss—That a villain is a villain is a villain. I wish it were that simple. But the truth is, evil people are capable of doing good things, just as good people are capable of doing evil things. As I mentioned earlier, I've never felt more seen than when watching "The Descendants" with my twins. The lines between good and evil can be so very grey.

Many of you have become more and more familiar with the harsh reality of your hero becoming a villain. There are thousands of us who have fallen prey to the promises of an MLM downline only to learn we only mattered as a number and not a person. I don't believe it's even a slight coincidence that there is a heavy overlap of religion and MLM "business owners". It's really easy for a seasoned soul winner to build a downline. Believe me. I was good at it.

On a larger scale, finally recognizing racism and police brutality is an extremely difficult thing for many of us to see. I'm deeply saddened it's taken until now to begin to call out the horrors of our society.

If I'm completely honest with you, it scares me. It scares me to think of people I've harmed because of what I thought they needed in their lives, or the hateful beliefs I've held. I've administered Ketamine before, and there may be a time it's called for in the future. I've been terrified and reluctant each time and I've only ever done it out of absolute safety of the patient, never anger. But I froze when I read about the two medics charged with manslaughter in the murder of Elijah McClain. I can't speak to their intentions, but they didn't take a life in the split second it takes to pull a trigger; their role was a matter of milligrams.

I should have noticed the role I play in systemic racism much sooner. But I don't carry a weapon. Patients usually trust me when I tell them I'm not a cop, that I'm only there for their health. I never saw myself as having the potential to become the villain—but, then again, do any of us? Sure, you may not be capable of plotting out an elaborate, premeditated murder; but in the heat of the moment, when reality is blinding and seconds are all you have, would your systemic beliefs save or destroy the person in front of you?

I wasn't raised thinking I wasn't racist. I knew I was racist, and I couldn't wait to vote for the people who stuck to the values of our Founding Fathers. Wisdom Booklet 49 teaches us that those elected are "representatives of his constituents, and in a very real sense, a representative of God…" Later in the paragraph, we read, "In a democracy such as the U.S. has become, this balance is destroyed by the concern for majority rule and minority rights. It seems that Americans today prefer representatives who are responsive to public opinion rather than men of character who will vote as their consciences dictate." (Note that this was not a quote from a historical book. This was written in 1987, yet women are still left out of government.)

These are the beliefs that originally shaped me. Honestly, if I hadn't taken the time to examine that my hateful beliefs had no place in my life, I don't know that I wouldn't have played an active role in ending an innocent life. I was raised to believe America was the greatest country on earth, that our Founding Fathers had all the right answers and that I was truly superior to those around me.

People ask how I can write a book about an abusive childhood without slandering my parents. This is how—because this is so much bigger than them. This is about being gaslit into abusive behavior that fosters a generation of hatred towards people who look, believe, or love differently than I do. Changing is uncomfortable, even painful, but you can do it. I believe in you.

We have to be willing to acknowledge that the ones we knew to be heroes may have been the villain to someone else. Only then can we move forward.

We have to be willing to admit that, perhaps, we are the villain in someone's story.

I've told you that I often hear songs as my personal soundtrack to my life. When my twins discovered "The Descendants," they had no idea why I was all about blasting "My Once Upon A Time" and dancing and singing at the top of our lungs. For them, it's fun. For me, it's incredibly healing.

> *"This is not your father's fairytale*
> *And no, it's not your mother's fault you fail*
> *So when your story comes to light*
> *Make sure the story that they write goes...*
> *Once upon a time, she fought the dragon*
> *Once upon a time, the beast was me*
> *Once upon a misspent youth*
> *She faced herself*
> *She spoke the truth*
> *That's how I see my once upon a time*
> *This time*
> *Life is not a storybook but life unfolds in chapters*
> *Turn the page and start to make amends*
> *There's no pre-written guarantee of "happily ever after"*
> *Step into your greatness before your story ends*
> *So when your story ends*
> *They'll say once upon a time a girl flew higher*
> *Once upon a time, she made things right*
> *Once upon a tie that binds*
> *She changed her heart*
> *To change their minds*
> *That's got to be my once upon a time*
> *This once upon a time*
> *I'll finally see my once upon a time*
> *This time"*

13

I Have Kept The Faith

"Well maybe there's a God above, but all I've ever learned from love is how to shoot somebody who outdrew ya. And it's not a cry that you hear at night, it's not somebody who's seen the light, it's a cold and it's a broken hallelujah."

—Leonard Cohen's "Hallelujah,"
the song I sing with my twins every night

E very night, when I'm mid "Dubs the Snugs" (double the snuggles) between my twins, we get to that verse in "Hallelujah" and I bask in the perfection of how well those words fit my current journey.

I'm not denying the existence of God; I believe in God and that the evil brought upon us by the cult was done by humans who take God's name in vain, not out of God's true love. They are the ones who fuel the hatred of the people created equally to them by God. They are the ones limiting the love all around them to fit their definition.

They are the ones who abused us and told us that abuse was out of love, teaching me only to shoot someone who outdrew me, how to survive. Without oversight, they were able to keep me hidden, and keep you from hearing the cries of the kids still trapped in that world. I didn't break free after a light-shining rhema; it's a slow, ongoing process. But here I am, cold and broken. Hallelujah, Amen.

Through writing this book, I've found my own version of faith, one that no man gets to define for me. (Cue "I Believe.") Way back in the beginning, I thanked you for holding my journey in your hands and I want you to know how true that is.

I began this book as someone who wanted to leave the world of homeschool as far behind me as possible and never look back. Oh, naive Homeschool Heather, how she refuses to vanish. All my life, I swore I'd never, ever homeschool my kids. Yet, there I am, back in my old world, reluctantly homeschooling along with the entire rest of the world through a global pandemic.

As much as I loathed every second of homeschooling my kids, I have to admit I'm grateful, both for the necessity and the timing. Do you know how surreal it is to start homeschooling while engrossed in the middle of writing the book on its damages? It changed my entire narrative—not to one in which I will ever condone the abusive practices that took place under the guise of love, but to one in which I recognize the value of an education best suited for each child as an individual.

One of the things I'd hear from the pulpit repeatedly was, "Everyone's a sinner. There's a price on sin. Jesus paid that price. Now, what are you gonna do about it?" My mind's Rolodex has flipped to that page often during my writing, that "What are you gonna do about it?" weighing heavy in my mind. I can't just put a book out there to complain that I missed out on a prom and got locked in a fundie extremist training center; I have to do something about it. I might not be able to change the world but, maybe, just maybe, I can change someone's world. I at least have to try.

But I need your help. You've already started by buying this book. That allowed me to donate a percentage of the profits to organizations committed to ending educational neglect in home-schooling, healing the trauma of religious abuse, and providing a path out for those who desire to leave but are truly trapped, either physically or logistically (many still trapped don't have records or IDs, making existence in the outside world nearly impossible). I'm so grateful to you, someone I may never know, for helping someone you may never know.

I challenge you now to get your bookmark and go help some-one in front of you, too. Hug your kid. Give your cash to some-one you pass on the street. Become friends with someone who dresses differently than you do. Visit one of the websites listed at the end of this chapter and learn how to get involved.

What is needed more than money is change, and that will only come when people step up and take action together. I needed voices like yours when I was a child. You could have been the hero I needed. Be one for the children who are still neglected and hidden. I can only point you toward a few, but there are so many places and ways to help.

One of the fabulous non-profits you're helping to support with your purchase of this book is The Coalition for Responsible Home Education (CRHE). I've had the privilege of speaking with two members of their staff, Chelsea, who is a public school alumni, and Jeremy, a homeschool alumni, for several hours about their mission and how best to provide you with helpful, actionable steps to take from here.

In the interest of not plagiarizing their entire website for a second book, please spend some time on their site (listed at the end of this chapter) to learn a plethora of both the homeschool positives and extreme tragedies of hidden homeschoolers. The site also provides many helpful resources on the best route to take for each of your children's educations. You'll also find help-ful articles, such as "40 Ways to Help Homeschooled Kids in Bad Situations."

If you do a quick internet search for homeschooler's rights, you'll find many cases from the Home School Legal Defense Association (HSLDA). I won't get into my personal feelings on their organization—because not getting sued is one of my favorite hobbies—but ATI families relied heavily on their work. While you'll find many individual cases on the rights of the parents, CRHE is the first organization I've encountered that fights for a child's right to an education.

Being a homeschool parent is one of the biggest commitments a person can make. It should never be taken lightly. But, all too often, it is, and it's often a choice made for the wrong reasons. CRHE brings to the forefront the rights of the child, something ATI not only denied us, but demanded we relinquish.

All my life, I'd heard I had to yield all of my rights, that I deserved nothing. Whatever education I was given was the one God had intended for me to have. When I spoke with Chelsea, that all changed. My Rolodex froze as she told me how they value the rights of children as full humans, with autonomy and valid feelings about the choices made regarding their life's direction. I was blown away by the idea of having the privilege of allowing your child to contribute heavily to the manner of education they receive. I'd never, ever thought of a child playing an active role in their own education and not just being parentified so they could homeschool their siblings.

Taking on a commitment of pouring all of yourself into all the educational, emotional, social, and health needs of a child makes it extremely easy to take on "homeschooling parent" as a full identity. That should be taken into great consideration when making educational choices.

I saw it happen to my mother when I asked to go to school when I was probably 7 or 8. She had poured all of herself into me, so my desire for an education beyond what she could provide was seen purely as my rejection of her as a mother, of everything she

had become. I remember spending hours comforting and reassur-
ing her after she became suicidal over my request. I loved her more
than anything and never wanted anyone else to be my mother. I
just wanted friends and a drama club. But she'd become unable to
separate herself as my teacher from herself as my mother.

Instead of exploring how to fulfill the needs I was expressing,
I learned that my mother's happiness depended on me suppressing my own desires. Everything I did became a reflection on her.
If I didn't grasp a concept the way it was being taught, I ended
up feeling too guilty to admit I didn't understand because it
meant my mother had failed. In my mind, being homeschooled
was a matter of my mother's life or death, so I never asked to go
to school again.

When I shared this experience in my discussion with Jeremy,
he confirmed my experience was far from unique. Far too often,
he hears this story of guilt from homeschool alumni who just
wanted their parents to stop crying over not being enough for
them. My mother didn't do any of that intending to abuse me.
It's strange to label what she saw as the greatest love she could
show me as psychological abuse, but it was.

People have asked my mother how she can support my
writing and online presence when she is painted as the villian.
Those people fail to see that her role was complex, and villains
can simultaneously be victims (My kids' obsession with watching
"The Descendants" has honestly been one of the most healing
avenues I've experienced thus far.) She's able to support me
because she understands accountability. I recognize she was
trapped by her own demons; all she wanted to do was save me
from the childhood pain she had experienced, but had no idea
how to protect me when she couldn't protect herself. Personally,
I think having a little sister who followed the straight-and-
narrow path softened the blow for my parents to admit they'd
raised a backslidden harlot. Thanks, Bups!

Last year, like many of you I had no choice but to homeschool. If I had stayed under that umbrella I'd had over me, I'd be in the same situation, forced to homeschool despite my desire or ability to provide a child with a full, valid academic, social, and enriching education, placing their needs above my own. I have no doubt I would have repeated the pattern of depression and suicidal fantasies if I'd been forced to homeschool the way my mother did. Do you know how fortunate I am that my kids are only 5? If they had been teenagers I would have been deeply deficient as their teacher, and I have far more resources than my mother did.

I'd have been lost this year without the wonders that are ABCmouse.com and Outschool.com. Thanks to these, my kids were able to join in with real live teachers in a Zoom classroom and follow a learning path I didn't have to create. I listened as those teachers taught with such skill, knowing exactly how to engage kids around the world to participate in a way that fit their individual comfort level. I've always held teachers on a secret pedestal but, after 2020, I will never not be in awe of their love and dedication to children who are not their own. Watching them, I knew, and my kids agreed that a school setting without me was the best thing for them. They are enrolled in public school for this fall.

On the flip side, my friend Sarah, who was a public school teacher before becoming a stay-at-home mom had the exact experience CRHE encourages. After a year in a pandemic and knowing she was capable of mental stability in a homeschool setting, she let each of her kids make the choice for themselves. Her son, who had always gone to school, ended up absolutely thriving in their mandated homeschool setting. Her daughter, who is a few days older than mine, has never been to school but is excited to go this fall. I did mute Sarah on social media for a minute because I felt incredibly inferior as a homeschooling mom, especially since

I'm one of the few who had actually experienced it for myself. I felt I should have been able to lead the world through this, since I'd been training my whole life for being locked in my house. Once I was comfortable seeing all my "worldly" friends homeschooling, I was in awe of her. Our contrast shouldn't have surprised me. The teacher in her will never die, which is evident by her shower curtains, home decor, and bottomless arts and craft ideas, themed for every holiday there is.

This was probably the first time I've ever been actively supportive of someone deciding to homeschool in a situation in which other enriching options are available. Between our "I miss you and love you and I don't know how to plan activities without you telling me when and where to show up" texts, we talked about how important it is to value our children as full people with choices. She told me, "I think it's important for them to have a say. Choice is so important, and I'm fortunate enough that I can stay home with him and do it! (Every day I hope I'm not ruining him.)" I feel like that's the key missing from the ATI experience. The focus was never on the parents doing the best they could for the kids' needs. It was only ever about the kids making the parents look good. It was never actually about us.

I told her how much I admired her constant self-reflection surrounding all of it, and she told me, "[He] also knows that no answer is permanent. He knows that, if come October he's missing school or it's not as fun, since [his sister] is at school, he can choose to go back to school. We are really trying to give them a voice."

Her words perfectly echo the conversation I had with Jeremy about how to know you're agreeing to the right choice. He said the best thing you can do, if you're fortunate enough to give your child multiple educational options, is to at least try it for a year and constantly reevaluate. If things really aren't working out as everyone hoped and you're miserable, you can always go back to the educational route best suited for your family and, most importantly, your child. He gave the example of being in a situation where a child and teacher may truly clash to the point of educational detriment, even though the child may otherwise thrive in a school setting. He's been able to witness firsthand the success of this situation in which a child was homeschooled for that year but kept in the social and extracurricular activities provided by the school.

It was well known to those of us in ATI that if there was a program in the school that parents cannot provide in a homeschool setting, such as a baseball team or drama club, the children are still fully allowed to participate in anything the town taxes would provide to public school children. This was something I knew to recite to anyone who questioned our lack of socialization. I was always told that I was legally welcome to participate in any town or school program I wanted, but I was never allowed to actually take advantage of it. The entire goal was only to get people to stop asking questions.

Because I was taught to recite this rhetoric every time I was challenged on the issue of socialization, I believed these laws, referred to as "Tebow Bills" (because of the football player Tim Tebow who was homeschooled), encompassed all of America. After speaking with Jeremy, I learned I was mistaken. He informed me that, although extracurricular participation for homeschoolers is law in about half the states, as of 2015, there are 20 states in which athletic associations have barred homeschoolers from participating. He went on to say, "CRHE actually lobbies for homeschoolers to have this access, but we're not always successful. Additionally, some states allow only limited access (sports but not drama, drama but not sports)."

When I spoke with Chelsea, I told her about my overwhelming feelings of inferiority as a homeschooler, especially when I saw the entire learning center my friend, Natalie, set up, completely customized to what worked best for her daughter. Natalie was even gracious enough to let us Zoom in for some of their lessons. Unfortunately, that ended up just making my pain of no longer living a few doors away from her unbearable, and her ability to transform into her new role as a teacher deepened my complex of never being able to succeed in educating my own kids. Natalie taught in a manner similar to that of the online teachers. I still attribute this to the fact that she had completed Kindergarten herself and I hadn't.

While it may be legal where many of us live, one of CRHE's policy recommendations is that parents only be allowed to home-school their children in grades the primary educating parent themselves have completed. (I'm sure most reasonable parents would be livid if they learned their child's public school teacher never met the requirements for the grade they are teaching. This is absolutely no different.) This is a huge issue for educationally neglected second-generation homeschoolers and those who were unable to complete high school. They may find themselves strug-gling to fill the gaps in their own education so they might success-fully continue an otherwise enriching homeschool experience.

What is truly alarming is when a parent is unaware of their own educational gaps, such as those who have been taught exclu-sively from a fundamentalist curriculum, as I was. Thankfully, ATI has less than one percent of second-generation families. I believe our discovery of our own educational neglect and abuse is one of the main reasons. We aren't capable of providing an education to someone when we never had one ourselves. The terrifying part of that, of course, is there are, in fact, still those families who choose to remain under the umbrella and embark on attempting to fulfill every single need a child has, when the parents are truly incapable of fulfilling those needs; yet, they either believe they are capable or don't value education enough for it to matter.

I do believe most families make the choice to homeschool out of love and, as Jeremy has pointed out and I've seen, it is possible to homeschool effectively. What many don't see is that loving someone doesn't mean you're not abusing them. Willingly robbing a child of an education is abuse. As Jeremy put it during our Zoom call, "Parents should be able to decide how to educate their children, not whether to educate them," and that includes parental ability. If CRHE had existed when I was a child, I'd like to think much of my trauma could have been avoided.

Navigating your way out of a cult and a world of extremism is so much more than the grandiose Disney princess version of sudden freedom and a happily ever after. It's lonely. Often, when people are in a world like I was, that's all they have. I am eternally grateful I was able to escape into the world of EMS, which paved a way for me to require gluing together some self-evaluated transcripts, earning a professional license, and being able to support myself.

Unfortunately, my case is not the norm for those of us raised in a world that fits under an umbrella. So many have the desire for more, for a higher or even a grade school education, a job, a path other than marriage and filling a quiver, but have no path to any of it. No one achieves the position of ultimate control of another human by being bad at manipulation. Our captors knew how to stay in control, even when we became adults. Many children in cults are born at home, meaning it's not difficult to keep the world from knowing that person ever even exists. There may not be a birth certificate, a social security card, a count on a census, medical care, anything.

In my discussion with Chelsea, I asked how many kids they believe are still hidden in these worlds. Her answer was bone-chillingly obvious: "We will never know." It's factually impossible to count them because they are hidden so well. The lack of standard oversight in America makes it all too easy to hide an entire life from view. The only reason we even know it's happening is because of those people brave enough to escape and speak up or if there is a crisis too devastating to hide but often too severe for rescuing.

In purchasing Lovingly Abused, you're also supporting The Amish Heritage Foundation, a non-profit to which those who have been hidden can turn to for help. Their website states they "... [E]nvision that one day education will be a federal right for all American and Native/Indigenous children, and Amish children will have the right to learn beyond the 8th grade and the right to learn about science, technology, engineering, math (STEM), and the arts". Currently, the Amish are legally allowed to cease education after 8th grade, regardless of the desires of the child. The AHF is committed to empowering women and children to decide their own future through education, providing logistical guidance on obtaining public records needed for American citizenship and employment, and offering support for those who have left a community, and perhaps an entire family, behind. Although their name suggests they serve specifically Amish, they provide resources to anyone who has been educationally neglected and robbed of the basic autonomy to create a life outside of oppression.

Walking away from an entire community is painful. Even though I'd left ATI, I kept going back to worship among the known child rapists and those admittedly on the brink of homicide, just like those mice in Chapter 6 that return to chaos over calm because it's all they've known. The unknown is terrifying, especially if you've never existed to the outside world around you.

Thanks to an Instagramer-turned-friend, I've discovered The Vashti Initiative, a non-profit created by fellow survivors of religious abuse, offering support and assistance to people like me, as we attempt to transition to a new world. Their volunteers offer assistance in educational pursuits and establishing employment while offering a community inclusive of those who have both left their faith and those like me who have left the abuse behind but kept their faith.

One of the deepest gaps I've felt after stepping out from under the umbrella was the void left from the community to which I'd felt I'd belonged. Walking away from your church family or, worse yet, being shunned can be devastating. Like an abusive relationship, even though you know you need to leave to survive, it's still incredibly painful. Before you follow my lead and try to fill the gaps the cult left with less extreme cults and join several MLMs, which are basically cults where the women are allowed to make money, take a breath and let yourself discover who you are for a while.

Because The Vashti Initiative is run by those who have already gone through the pain of leaving abuse, they have created ways to hold on to the positives of Sunday gatherings via a monthly virtual Sunday Support group. I've been pointing many survivors to groups like this recently, as the pandemic has thankfully allowed many people I love to see the hypocrisy of their Spiritual leaders, whose maskless actions and packed pews during the height of our country's spiking death toll proved they don't actually care about the wellbeing of those around them. I've seen the most genuinely Spiritual people I know walk away from their church family out of their love for their neighbor and their value of life, but still feel the weight of the grief that accompanies the loss of their entire community.

I know that many who have been deconstructing religion, like myself, and have left their faith completely, but I haven't. My "substance of things hoped for" still remains as I've sifted through my broken hallelujahs, watching as men twist any words they want just to fit their agenda, always circling back to believing that the God I've loved from the beginning has been one of love the entire time. I am capable of believing in science and in a loving God all at once, just like you are capable of tremendous things. I've found exponential comfort in learning about the vast complexity of the universe and nature, all the aspects that had been kept from me, for fear I'd begin to doubt God.

It's been the opposite. It made me angry at those who always told me not to limit God; I can't help but wonder why they would limit God to only a few thousand years. I don't see why believing in evolution has to mean not believing in a God so wonderfully, humanly incomprehensible that God created life to change in this way. Opening my mind to the beautiful, forbidden worlds of astronomy or environmentalism, things specifically taught as false in the Wisdom Booklets, have only drawn me closer to an omnipotent, magnificent God. Many of you who have embarked on the journey of deconstruction as I have, have turned away from God altogether. Many still feel completely torn.

We are each on our very own uncomfortable journey through this. Those who recognize and respect those differences are the ones who have helped me the most. Thank you. It takes a great deal of work to maintain respect over indifference, to acknowledge the trauma and eventual healing of others. I am happy to share my story with you, but I've given up the exhausting goal of trying to convince people to align their religious beliefs with mine, and that is a peace unlike any I have ever known.

Right now, all I ask is for you to help make the world a kinder place. There are nightmares all around us, but educational neglect is one we are capable of waking up from. Making the changes necessary to protect those right in front of us from being lovingly abused is going to be hard. But I promise you, it will be worth it all.

2 Timothy 4:7 I have fought a good fight, I have finished my course, I have kept the faith.

To learn more, please visit:
Responsiblehomeschooling.org
Amishheritage.org
Vashtiinitiative.org

Acknowledgments

This book would not have been possible without the support of those who have taken this journey along with me. -In no particular order:

Liz, it all began with you. When you asked if you could write your report for school on me it gave me the idea that mine was a story worth telling. Thank you for not being afraid to be friends with the weird kid next door. Thank you for still talking to me after I ran out of your house thinking you were trying to take over my mind by teaching me yoga. Thank you for waiting by the radio to record "I want it that way" and "Bye Bye Bye" on a secret cassette tape for me so I could have one thing that was normal. Thank you for co-choreographing a "secret" handshake (I'm hoping muscle memory allows us to drop everything and do it flawlessly when I finally see you in person). Thank you for taking me back as a friend after I disowned you for getting a tattoo. You taught me how to be a friend, and you taught me that friends can forgive. You were my first friend in this world, and I will love you forever. Please can we get friendship tattoos?

Hope, aka "Bups", my little sister. Thank you for being my very first audience. I just love you so much it hurts. Thank you for letting me use our childhood photos for this book. It's impossible to tell my story without you. Thank you for never being fazed by my habits of dressing like a princess at the mall, singing along to all the Disney songs in the car, and letting me steal your clothes. Thank you for being the good kid. Seriously, they needed one of us not to be a disappointment, so thanks for taking that one for the team. Thank you for picking your niece's middle name when I couldn't think anymore. Thank you for showing me it's possible to scream at someone and then love them even more when you stop. I love you more than you'll ever possibly know, and I don't know how to show it, so I wrote you a book.

My parents, Thank you for skipping chapter 8. It's better for everyone this way. Thank you for being open to processing the extremely harsh reality of learning that your child is rejecting most of the standards you'd adopted as the only way to live. I imagine this is the most difficult book you'll ever read, and I hope you find healing in reading it, as I've found in writing it. Thank you for listening as I've shown you the damage ATI has done. Thank you for rearranging your house once a month for the past 5 years so the twins and I can take over and I can continue to work my dream job. Thank you to my mom for sharing her story, allowing me to see how we all got here, and have a deeper understanding of trauma rather than anger. I love you.

Gramma, for being my original editor from the moment I learned to talk; "What, are you writing a book? Leave that chapter out." Although I doubt I could confine Gramma to a single chapter.

Michelle Foley, You poetic, noble, land mermaid. Thank you for being the Ann to my Leslie in every possible way. I can't believe I'm lucky enough to be your friend. When I had to write a paper on soul friends, you were instantly the one who came to mind. I sobbed the whole time I wrote it as most people sob during their wedding vows. Thank you for being the most passionately honest person I know. I miss you so much and I love that being a country apart hasn't dimmed our excitement of hearing each other's voices. Thank you for letting your phone go to voicemail when I call because you know neither of us has time to talk for the inevitable 3 hours we'll be on the phone telling each other how fucking unstoppable and beautiful the other is. I love that our text conversations last weeks because we are so genuinely happy the other one didn't write back because she set technology boundaries and is prioritizing their mental health. I miss you so much and I know you're going to cry when you finally hold this book in your hands. Knowing there is someone out there who loves me as much as you do now has me openly weeping in a coffee shop next to the grocery store. Let' go back to saying "yay!"

Rory and Abby, for teaching me how to snuggle and type at the same time. I love being your mommy, and I love who you are.

My husband, for inspiring my unquenchable thirst for always needing to learn more, forever. For being a part of my real-time deconstruction and guest staring in my posts. Thank you for showing me how high the bar of how humans should act should actually be. Thank you for being my area of refuge, and for not throwing the piano in the fire. After deconstructing through typing this book I know I don't owe you thanks for marrying me, an adulterous harlot, even though I automatically typed it.

Anna, thank you for being the one who wasn't afraid of how uncool sitting next to me at church looked. Thank you for coming to my birthday parties and for including me when no one else did. Thank you for growing up into someone I'm proud to know. Thank you for showing me that no one gets to define my faith and that you can still worship in pants.

Megan Wooding, author of "Dear Sister", Thank you for being exactly who you are. Who would have thought when we were 6 and fighting over a swing because we were both the bossiest that we would grow up to embrace and foster that bossiness in each other. I think I read something somewhere about iron sharpening iron or something like that... I think we ran with that. You went from the friend I was forced to have because of our parents to the only one in the world I would trust to photograph my book cover. Thank you for the honor of being a part of your book and promoting the essence of support over competition. Thank you for taking every design concept I had in my mind and making it a reality for this cover. You knew the depths of what every detail meant to me, and you captured all of it. Cheers to tent stakes and being bossy together!

Sandi Sharp, Thank you for being the first person I ever knew in real life who was brave enough to write a book, let alone use the word "vagina" in it. You showed me that I never have to accept no for an answer, I just have to keep looking. Thank you for handing me your manuscript when I was 14 years old when most people around us thought it was "too mature" for me due to medically anatomical details. Your manuscript was the first time I learned that marriage was about having a partner, not about meeting a man's every desire no matter your suffering. You gave me the courage to speak up and tell my Drs when I knew they missed something. Thank you for inspiring me to advocate for women, to be a better caregiver, and most of all, to tell my story.

"Paula", Thank you for being the best therapist on earth. I wouldn't be here without you. Thank you for making me "sit with the feeling", even though you knew it made me project those feelings at you. Thank you for getting me to where I am, and validating the absolute shit that was my education. I'm not sure of the protocol here, but if you want to tell people you are the one who therapied a cult out of me, I'm all about you taking credit for the good parts of me. You're irreplaceable (trust me, I've tried and continue to fail). I hope reading this shows you how truly powerful your work is.

Dr. Danielle Ziehl, for taking me shopping for my infamous first jeans when we were baby EMTs. Thank you for showing me how to command a room and how to conserve the number of fucks I give a day.

Claire Wasserman, author and founder of "Ladies Get Paid", Thank you for being a huge inspiration, and so generous with your time and help with advice, edits, pulling the idea for my introduction from one sentence over a phone call, drafting a full proposal, and for believing in me from the beginning. Thank you for showing my daughters you don't have to decide between bright pink nail polish and building a business.

Elizabeth, Thank you for being the worst Family Coordinator ATI has ever known.

Amanda McCauley, for never being afraid to tell me to get out of my own head and just freaking write, and for the hours you've spent letting me talk things out. You showed me how powerful telling your story can be, and I'm absolutely honored and thrilled to start typing yours! The world needs to hear your story, your brilliant outlook on your surroundings, and most of all, how fucking hilarious you are! I love you and I couldn't have done this without you. Find Amanda's blog at AmandasQuadQuips. blogspot.com

Natalie, I've loved you since the first time I met you and you were in the middle of writing a parody to demand Sen. Collins stop being terrible. Thank you for telling the internet trolls how much of a catch I actually am, and for being the baddest ass future politician I know. You're the one I call when I'm screaming and no one else will understand me, let alone validate me. Thank you for being 1 of the 2 people on earth I trusted to get this book printed if for some reason I couldn't. I miss you and I love you.

Sarah and Dr. Matt, for truly being friends who have become family. Thank you for continuing to hang out with us after we invited you over to watch our babies try to get Cheerios into their mouths, because that's the coolest party trick we have. Thank you for having late-night conversations about being able to believe in science and in God. Thank you for normalizing saying "I love you" to friends and to friends' kids. Thank you, Sarah, for being the one who debunked ATI's lies and showed me how genuinely and selflessly teachers can love their students.

Daniel, I waited until I wasn't in a coffee shop to type this because I know I'll cry. Thank you for being one of the very first internet Exer friends I made on this journey. Thank you for helping me unlock painful and normal-to-us memories that otherwise may not have made it onto these pages. Thank you for making it easy to bounce ideas off you because I don't have to stop and explain cult-speak. I wish I could hold your book in my hands. You have immense wisdom to share. You deserve to have your dream immortalized and it just fucking sucks that I can't possibly give enough of my platelets to give the world more time with you in it. I can't believe I'm never going to get to give you a hug or meet you in person. I promise you will be the one I think of every time I have that needle in my arm. I am clinging to the hope that you will have a book out there one day in which you can live forever, but until then, I hope you enjoy living here in mine. To everyone reading this, please donate blood, sign up for the marrow registry, be an organ donor. You never know how many lives will be touched by the one you helped extend.

Alex the best PA I've ever known, Amanda R, Amy, Courtney, Dr. Eliza, Heather R, Dr. Jack, Jessi, Jess A, B, F, & M, John, Kate, Dr. Katie C, Aunt Katie, Dr. Kelly C, Kelly M, Keziah, Kristina, Kristine, Lauren B, Lindsey, Mallory, MaryKate, Melissa R, Michelle M, Paul, Rachel N, Sam AF, Sam N, Sarah S, Stevie, Taylor, and anyone I may have missed, for either being cameos in the turning points of my journey and/or for reading sporadic chapters I've anxiously sent you (or made you read in front of me so I could read your face) so you could tell me nice things and make me confident enough to hit "send" on my final manuscript.

My favorite places to write are coffee shops and restaurants, and each one has made me feel more at home than any address I've ever had. In Maine, I loved Elements and Run of the Mill. Rachael, Thank you for being the ultimate playgroup mom by day and bartender who makes me order vegetables with my martinis at my corner window by night. You are the reason I'm no longer afraid to make mom friends. You showed me being a mom doesn't mean I have to lose myself.

It took me over a year after moving to New York to find a corner of the world that felt like my own. I finally found SkyTop, where the owner, Serena knows my name and where the chapter I was going to omit became a reality inspired by simultaneous servings of fancy wine from Steve, and espresso from Eli, the homeschooled barista who still bring my orders to my table even though I told them they already earned a thank you credit. Thank you to every cafe who has provided me a place to create.

Alica M, for being a total babe; the small town girl who made it in the big city, aka my hero. Thank you for saying "Why didn't you call me?!?!?" when you have expert advice to give on how to vet an interviewer but I'm afraid to bother you. Thank you for doing mock interviews with me without being asked. Thank you for your late night confidence boosting texts and for showing me that my writing doesn't have to fit anyone else's style. Find Alicia's blog at SuburbiaHatesSidewalks.com

Shannon, for being the one person in town who had a broken umbrella that would come in handy for something someday. Little did you know you'd meet a friend who needed to tear it apart with her high heels and put it on a book cover.

Brandon for taking a chance on a friendship with the weird girl.

Nick, for having no idea what you were getting into when I told our boss we needed to be partners, and for spending years supportively reading every single Word doc I've sent you as my thoughts finally evolved into this book.

Lauren, for being the best cousin ever. Thank you for knowing exactly when to have Cheetos sent to my house. Thank you for being exactly as weird as I am, for marrying me, and for yes, and-ing pretty much every plan I ever have.

My in-laws for buying me a new laptop after I thought I'd have to stop writing this when my old borrowed one suddenly stopped working. My father-in-law has been asking every day if he made it into the book yet, even though I keep telling him this isn't the book you want to be in. Now I'll finally be able to tell him he made the cut.

"My Teenage Crush", Thank you for reviewing the chapter where you are featured, and for agreeing with me on what parts of the story should stay omitted.

Sadie Carpenter and Gavri'el HaCohen, Thank you for creating and inviting me to be a guest on your podcast, "Leaving Eden", which has made my life much easier in that I can just tell my husband to play the latest episode and it saves us the time of having to have the exact same conversation about how deep the brainwashing went. Thank you for directing me to Evan and The Vashti Institute; thanks to you, they'll be getting 5% of my profits.

Jess and Kit, creators and co-hosts of the podcast "Leaving The Village", thank you for putting this brilliant podcast into the world! You are helping more Exers than you'll ever know. Thank you for making me feel seen and most of all for having me on not once, but twice! Thank you for sharing your stories, and for supporting mine!

Annie, creator of the podcast, "Escape: Leaving Hell Behind" and founder of the soon-to-exist non-profit "Succeeding After

Escaping: helping those who leave cults, high-demand religions, and possibly even eventually non-religious abusive situations", for having me as a guest on your podcast and for giving so many survivors a safe platform in which to tell their stories.

Evan from The Vashti Initiative and Jeremy and Chelsea from CRHE, thank you for giving me so much of your time for interviews, and your crucial work in helping to change someone's world.

Heather King, for being an extremely vulnerable ex-homeschooler online and inspiring me to get my GED after this goes to print.

Caeresa, for my serendipity mittens and connecting me with Lorna! You are shining proof of why I love making friends out of complete strangers. When society would call for a mere business transaction, we went beyond that and you shaped so much of this book.

Lorna Oppedisano, editor extraordinaire, you are magical. You took the idea behind my words and turned them into what I couldn't quite articulate. Your comments interspersed between edit notes made accepting constructive critiques so much more palatable. I doubt you had any idea when you signed onto this project what you were in for, or how many times you would have to tell me to remove the word "that" from my sentences, but you stuck with me. I am forever grateful for your commitment and belief in Lovingly Abused from the moment you signed on. Thank you for answering emails on your honeymoon even though I told you not to. I am honored to have had you play such a crucial role in making my dream a reality and I hope you aren't afraid to sign on for the prequel I'm already planning! Thank you especially for your generosity when I threw one more surprise chapter at you after our contract was finished. Instead of drawing me up a completely deserved invoice, you asked me to give your final check to the non-profits to whom my sales profits will benefit. That level of selflessness is what makes your contributions to this book magical. You proved this was more than a job for you; that you truly believe in the work you do. I can't wait to meet you in person and finally buy you a coffee!

Nicole and Kristin, for being there step by step through the process of turning this into a real live book, and for not ghosting me after I accidentally told you I loved you after our first phone interview.

Kristen and Chad, Words will never be enough to thank you for all the work you put into making this final project exactly what it needed to be. Thank you for giving up 3 entire days (and nights, thanks to breastfeeding) binge reading this entire book, and pointing out everything I missed. When I emailed the final manuscript to a handful of trusted friends, to have some extra eyes on the final product, I never expected you two to step up the way you did. Thank you for continuing to read even when the torment of nightmares and vomiting meant I had to stop reading my own book. One from The World, one from the cult, and complete strangers, you instantly began working together to make my dream a reality, and now I'm crying again. Your devotion to this will never be matched. Who needs an help meet when I have you two?

About the Author

Heather Heath was raised in the extreme fundamentalist homeschool organization, The Advanced Training Institute, or ATI. Despite having no accredited transcripts and being told girls didn't need to go to college, she graduated from Connecticut's paramedic program and later earned an A.S. while parenting infant identical twins...which led to her tendency of skipping mugs and sticking a straw directly into the coffee pot. Out of pandemic necessity, she has now been on both the student and teacher sides of homeschooling and would not like to relive either experience. Heather has been a guest on the podcasts "Leaving The Village" and "Escape: Leaving Hell Behind." She was interviewed in The New York Post, as well as for the book *Dear Sister* by M. Wooding. She has upcoming interviews on the podcast "Leaving Eden", and The Dr. Oz Show, and has been signed for a documentary film on the hidden world of cults. Heather is a popular blogger and (mostly) enjoys an ever-growing community on social media as @ BacksliddenHarlot. Her husband's career previously brought the family to live in Maine, and currently, they reside in New York. Heather still works as a paramedic in Connecticut, which inspired the location for the cover photo. This is her first book (and she's really excited about it). HeatherGraceHeath.com

Printed in November 2021
by Rotomail Italia S.p.A., Vignate (MI) - Italy